THE POPES AND SOCIAL PROBLEMS

THE POPES AND SOCIAL PROBLEMS

An Impartial Account of the Teaching Contained in their Encyclical Letters

BY

J. W. POYNTER

(Author of *Rome, Christendom, and a " League of Churches " ; The Second Summer ; Forgotten Crimes ;* etc.)

LONDON

WATTS & CO.

5 & 6 JOHNSON'S COURT, FLEET STREET, E.C.4

First published 1949

262.1324
P877
114029

Printed and Published in Great Britain by C. A. Watts & Co. Limited,
5 & 6 Johnson's Court, Fleet Street, London, E.C.4

PREFACE

It seemed to the compiler of this volume that a very useful purpose would be served by setting out in adequate form, so far as space allowed, a correct summary of the teaching of modern Roman Pontiffs on the political and social problems of our age. After all, the Popes, though they reign amidst a divided Christendom, and many millions of Christians reject their authority, still exercise great moral and secular influence. Their voice is listened to with reverence by Catholics all over the world; they speak for an ancient and venerable tradition; even very many non-Catholics regard them with deepest respect. What they say is of grave importance—and they have said a lot on the social and political problems of the last seventy or so years. It is timely, therefore, to produce an accurate summary of what they have said.

Such summary, however, if it is to be of any real use, must be impartial. There are plenty of attacks on the Popes; there are plenty of defences of them. What is needed is an account, in a succinct form, and without controversial bias, of what they themselves have said. Readers can then form their own judgment. This small book is an attempt to supply that want. It simply shows what the Popes teach. As to the quotations from the Encyclicals, some have been made directly by the present writer; others are as given in officially-published Catholic English versions.

The original Encyclicals (generally in Latin, but not always) are printed in the official " Acts of the Apostolic See " (*Acta Apostolicae Sedis*), and occasionally, in very important cases, in the Vatican newspaper, *Osservatore Romano*. They are not easily accessible in England, but the more outstanding documents and other Papal statements are translated and published in the Catholic periodicals of the various countries. Most Encyclicals on current problems are obtainable in English from the Catholic Truth Society, London: so the quotations in the present book are readily verifiable.

Though this little book does not express controversial opinions of its compiler, one general remark may be made. The ideal of the Popes seems clearly to be that of a return to what may be called the " pre-Reformation " system, in so far as Catholicism then was supreme—though without the evils which also existed, by reason, as the Popes would say, of sin. (Yet, after all, the human race with which they would be dealing would be much the same as the human race of older days!). Such an ideal of restored Catholic supremacy may appear, in our age, impossible indeed! The ideas and practices of Protestantism and Secularism are so impregnably dominant that a wish to return to a Catholic organization of society seems like wishing for the moon. Yet—who knows? If a new war came, civilization would collapse. Perhaps the Papacy would be the only effective power which would survive. If so, it has its doctrine ready by which to reconstruct the social community. It happened after the fall of the old Roman Empire. Might it not occur again, " history repeating itself "? Of course, the Popes would not desire to regain power by such a terrible process; but they would not refuse power if it became accessible. They would deem it a duty " to restore the world on right lines." Again, they may simply hope to exercise what influence they can in a confused world. In any case they have put forward their teachings, and this book endeavours to make clear, in brief synopses, what those teachings are.

There can be little doubt, however, that, should the Papal ideals ever be translated into reality (a contingency, whether or not it be impossible, at any rate seems remote), then what by our modern world is understood as Liberalism, free progress on secular lines, and Rationalism, would be destroyed, and the world would again be ruled by a theocratic polity as, to so considerable an extent, it was in the Middle Ages. The Papal Encyclicals, etc., are persuasive, eloquent, and appealing, and largely embody humanitarian teachings and projects which all will admit as admirable. Nevertheless, the ultimate aim underlying the whole Papal philosophy is that of placing society under supreme religious control. As Leo XIII said in his Encyclical *Libertas* (quoted in this book): As to " liberty of speech," " liberty of the Press," and " liberty of teaching," those are evil unless guided by the Law of God as expounded by the Church: for " the liberty of which We have been speaking is greatly opposed to reason, and tends absolutely to pervert men's minds." And again, Pius XII in his Allocution (speech), *Ancora una Volta*, to the Sacred College of Cardinals, June 1, 1946:—

" A general sense of uneasiness, discontent, and distrust poisons the atmosphere, frustrates high endeavour, dulls the impulse of good will, stifles the spirit of generosity and sacrifice without which there can be no real reconstruction . . . . At a time when material jealousies and rivalries are threatening to engulf humanity; when in the heat of conflict a transitory common interest of the purely economic or political order tends to obliterate the sentiment of true

Christian brotherhood; when the forces of revolution and atheism make it their object to drive the deluded masses like a flock of sheep, disguising under false appearances the goal (especially in the moral and religious sphere) to which they are being led—at such a time it is more than ever necessary for the Church, like a lighthouse, to send forth its bright and guiding beam, shedding the light of Christ on the course that must be followed, and clearly showing the limits to the right or left of which there are rocks and whirlpools that threaten shipwreck . . . . But this is no reason for being dismayed or disheartened, or for losing sight of the real situation as a whole. And so We [the Pope] shall never tire of saying to all Our children, and to all who share their sentiments: ' Take courage; be of good heart. You are numerous, more numerous than would appear . . . God is with you! ' "

A very eloquent statement of the Papal theory can be found in John Henry Newman's *Apologia* (Everyman's Library edition, pp. 220–5), from which the following may be quoted:—

" Supposing then it to be the will of the Creator to interfere in human affairs, and to make provision for retaining a knowledge of Himself, so definite and distinct as to be proof against the energy of human scepticism: in such a case—I am far from saying that there was no other way—but there is nothing to surprise the mind, if He should think fit to introduce a power into the world, invested with the prerogative of infallibility in religious matters . . . . And the initial act of that divinely-commissioned power is of course to deliver her challenge and to defy the enemy."

Of course, this theory depends for its validity on the ability of the Catholic Church to prove her claim to be that divinely-accredited teacher. Students of history will not fail to discover formidable objections: The real or apparent doubtfulness of the origins of the Popedom in the enclouded early days of Christianity; the numerous anti-Popes who have (and not only in 1378–1417!) divided the Church's unity; the Church's own association with so much of the very evils she is alleged to oppose: and so on. This is not the place to discuss the question, but the Rationalist view is forcibly expressed in W. K. Clifford's *Ethics of Belief* (Watts, 1947; Thinker's Library):—

" A revival of any form of sacerdotal Christianity would be a matter of practice and not of theory. The system which sapped the foundations of patriotism in the old world; which well-nigh eradicated the sense of intellectual honesty and seriously weakened the habit of truth-speaking, which lowered men's reverence for the marriage-bond by placing its sanctions in a realm outside of nature instead of in the common life of men, and by the institutions of monasticism and a celibate clergy; which stunted the moral sense of the nations by putting a priest between every man and his conscience; this system, if it should ever return to power, must be expected to produce worse evils than those which it has worked in the past. The house which it once made desolate has been partially swept and garnished by the free play gained for the natural goodness of men. It would come back accompanied by social diseases perhaps worse than itself, and the wreck of civilized Europe would be darker than the darkest of past ages."

Readers may be referred to two further books, one Catholic, the other not: *The Key to the World's Progress*, by C. Stanton Devas (Longmans, 1909), and *The Catholic Church Against the Twentieth Century*, by Avro Manhattan (Watts, 1947). Meanwhile, the pre-eminent fact is that *the Catholic Church is opposed* à outrance *to the conception of " secular, lay, Rationalist progress," and would destroy it and substitute a rule of society based on Catholic ecclesiastical ideals*. (See Encyclical *Quas Primas*, summarized at end of this book). Thus a vital struggle of principle is involved.

J. W. P.

Highbury,
   London, N.5.
      January, 1948.

CONTENTS

INTRODUCTION

THE famous nineteenth-century French Dominican friar and orator, Père Lacordaire, once gave in the Cathedral of Notre Dame, Paris, a notable sermon on the perpetual steadfastness of the Roman Pontificate. He depicted the rise and fall of empires, kings, and other merely earthly potentates: how they had achieved power, shone in glory for a time, and then had disappeared. With these he contrasted the Papacy: ever the same, triumphing over all vicissitudes, always remaining the vigilant and unsubduable guardian of divine truth. " Kings rise, kings fall, empires rise, empires fall, republics come and go," he proclaimed; " yet all the time, in a place called the Vatican, stands an old man with a parchment in his hand, who says, ' I am the guardian of revelation; here stand I, God with me; the things of this earth come and go, but here at all times I remain, God's ambassador. I never change.' "

This, of course, was oratory. It is not correct to say that the Papacy has never changed. The Pope who was represented at the Council of Nicaea, in the fourth century, only by two simple priests, and who, so far as records can discover, did not actually in a formal manner confirm that Synod's decrees, evidently was in a very different position from the nineteenth-century Pius IX, who defined, by his own plenary authority, the doctrine of the Immaculate Conception of the Blessed Virgin Mary as being a dogma divinely revealed, to be believed steadfastly by all the faithful, and who, at the Vatican Ecumenical Council, sixteen years later (1870), made, in his own person (" the

1

Sacred Synod approving "), the definition that all Popes are and have been infallible when they speak *ex cathedra.*

There was nevertheless an essential truth in the eloquent friar's words. Although the Papacy has passed through outward changes, and has been subject, as are all things on earth, to a process of gradual evolution (with setbacks and recoveries), yet beneath all such mutations it has preserved a substantial identity. How, then, does it stand in our present, mid-twentieth-century, tragic, revolutionary age? What are the principles which it proclaims in relation to the grave political and social problems of that age? And has its religious and/or political influence increased or diminished? (Consult Newman's *Essay on Development.*)

With respect to political prestige there can be little doubt as to the answer to the last of these questions. The power of the Papacy to influence secular affairs has lessened notably during the last seventy or so years. When the 1870 Vatican Council was held, its deliberations were watched eagerly and often with gloomy forebodings by Europe's statesmen. The decree on the Infallibility of the Roman Pontiff was regarded by many of those statesmen (including our own W. E. Gladstone) as being likely to affect dangerously the civil allegiance of citizens by placing it, to a perilous degree, at the call of arbitrary Papal orders. In our own times, on the other hand, though the political action of the Papacy is powerful in some countries (such as Spain and, strange to say, the United States of America), yet in others, where it used to be predominant, it now has to operate but as one party among several; and, as regards the general attitude of world-statesmen, those people seem relatively indifferent to the Papacy.

We must not be too hasty, however, in drawing conclusions from such an apparent state of affairs. Power may decrease in some ways and yet continue, or even increase, in others. The development of the Pontificate since 1870 illustrates this fact. In overt political power it seems to have lost much. When the then new (and, as few observers at that time would have predicted, so short-lived by destiny!) Kingdom of Italy deprived Pius IX, in 1870, of the position of King of the Papal States, that Pontiff retired (and his successors were to follow his example) into scornful solitude in the Vatican, declining to admit the new state of affairs as legitimate. In their very solitude, however, their religious influence increased. The Catholic world regarded them as august victims of a usurping tyranny. A halo began to crown them which had been far less evident when they had been, not Popes only, but also temporal rulers with all the visible defects of that position.

The Popes addressed themselves to a form of propaganda which, though not new, they greatly augmented after 1870: the issuing of Encyclical Letters addressed to the whole Catholic Church through its hierarchy of bishops. The 1870 decree on Papal Infallibility had stated that the Popes are, by divine protection, immune from error when they define a doctrine of faith or morals " from the chair " (*ex cathedra*); but no precise list has ever been compiled of exactly which Papal declarations, during the centuries, are comprised within that category. It might apply to many, or to relatively few, such declarations.

What has been one consequence of that uncertainty? As this or that of many Papal pronouncements may be perhaps infallible or perhaps not, it remains to a great extent open to Catholic theologians, in theory, to regard it as probably not infallible. Nevertheless, as being a solemn utterance of the highest authority in the Church, it must be accepted with reverence and believed " with interior religious assent " (Addis and Arnold, *Catholic Dictionary*, ed. 1917, article, " Encyclicals "). Moreover, it is often possible, or even probable, that this or that declaration may be within the 1870 conditions of infallibility. Thus since 1870 the Popes have been able to publish a mass of teaching not all, or even most, of which, in theory, is binding as articles of faith, but which is nevertheless binding to some extent, and in any case is entitled to the highest reverence. This ambiguity has been utilized to the full by the Popes, since 1870, through their frequent putting forth of Encyclical Letters.

The most copious writer of those documents was the long-lived Leo XIII, who was Pontiff for over a quarter of a century, and died in 1903. His Encyclicals covered almost all aspects of public affairs, secular as well as religious. In theology he condemned Anglican Ordinations as, from the Catholic point of view, " absolutely null and utterly void." He promoted devotion to the Blessed Virgin Mary. He encouraged the study of the Scholastic Philosophy, especially as expounded by St. Thomas Aquinas. He was busy, however, in other matters as well as those chiefly theological or philosophic. He put forward a mass of teaching as to temporal politics and sociology. He condemned Socialism, Communism, Anarchism, and " false Liberalism." He proclaimed, in considerable detail, the historic Papal conception of the right relations of Church and State. He dealt also with numerous special social problems.

The successors of Leo have followed his example, though, as a consequence of their shorter reigns and of the more stormy events in the world of their times, to a less extent. Their Encyclicals have confirmed Leo's teaching and have supplemented it.

Thus since 1870 the Popes have published a great quantity of solemn teaching on almost all subjects, and it has been enforced on Catholics with the highest sanctions of conscience short of actually being declared binding on faith. As the Roman Catholic Church ramifies in almost every country, and has a membership of many millions, this propaganda must have great effect. To a considerable extent it must compensate for the loss of much overt political power. We shall not be concerned, in this book, with the truth or otherwise of the Papal doctrines. That question would call for separate treatment. Our principal aim here is to summarize and set forth accurately the teaching of the Encyclicals.

THE ENCYCLICALS IN GENERAL

THE London *Catholic Times*, June 14, 1935, said: "The Papal Encyclicals on social questions are like the Bible: they need an expert commentator . . . Papal Encyclicals without notes and commentaries, of at least a semi-official character, are not a safe guide to the uninstructed, whilst the form in which they are drawn up detracts from their value as propaganda. An ardent Protestant social student, to whom we presented a copy of *Rerum Novarum*, returned it with the comment that he could not get through it. It was as heavy and technical, he said, as an Act of Parliament."

There is a good deal of truth in this, but it is an exaggeration. Encyclicals are generally—though not always—written in Latin; they deal with technical matters, and of course they call for some previous knowledge in the reader—but, on the whole, their language is plain and straightforward. They are known by the first one, two, or three words in the Latin original: for example, the Encyclical of Pius X (September, 1907) on "the doctrine of the Modernists," is called *Pascendi Dominici Gregis* ("On feeding the Lord's Flock") because those were its first words. Encyclicals are addressed as a rule to the whole Catholic Church through the bishops, and begin usually with this greeting: "To Our Venerable Brethren, the Patriarchs, Primates, Archbishops, Bishops, and Other Local Ordinaries in Peace and Communion with the Apostolic See, Pope [name]. Venerable Brethren, Health and Apostolic Benediction." The Encyclical then goes

direct to its subject, and ends with a blessing and the date;
thus: " We impart to you, Venerable Brethren, your clergy
and people, and to the whole Catholic world, the Apostolic
Benediction.   Given at Rome, at St. Peter's [or wherever
else it was issued], on the . . . day of . . . [year], the
. . . th of Our Pontificate."   The name " Encyclical " (from
Greek *enkuklikos*, " general ") means simply " a circular
letter."   These documents are to be distinguished from
Bulls (Latin, *bulla*, " seal," because of the leaden seal
attached to them)—which treat of an affair of some particular
part of the Church; from Briefs (short letters); and from
the *Motu Proprio* (" of his own motion ") form of utterance
—the last named being some spontaneous address or
other statement on a special occasion.   Encyclicals are
given the widest possible publicity by being (when this can
be done) read in churches, translated into the vernacular
of various countries and published in the Catholic Press;
issued, in translations, as pamphlets; and commented on
by Catholic writers.

Before beginning our summary of the chief Encyclicals on
social subjects issued after 1870, we may allude to a special
subject: the opposition of Popes to Freemasonry and
other secret societies.   Such associations became very
active before and after the French Revolution at the end of
the eighteenth century—especially in France, Italy, and
Spain—and the Papacy (even before the Revolution) condemned them utterly.   For example, Pope Clement XIII
(Encyclical *In Eminente*, 1738): " Under an outward
semblance of natural probity, which they require, and
which they regard as sufficient . . . , the Freemasons have
established certain laws and statutes binding themselves to
each other . . .; but, since crime ultimately betrays itself,
their assemblies have become to the faithful such objects of

suspicion that every good man now regards affiliation to them as a certain indication of wickedness and perversion. . . . Wherefore, . . . for the sake of the peace and safety of civil governments and the spiritual safety of souls, . . . to each and all of the faithful of Christ, of whatever state, grade, condition, or order, We ordain stringently and in virtue of holy obedience, that they shall not under any pretext enter, propagate, or support, the aforesaid societies, known as Freemasons, or otherwise named ; that they shall not be enrolled in them, affiliated to them, or take part in their proceedings, assist them, or afford them in any way counsel, aid or favour, publicly or privately, directly or indirectly, by themselves or by others in any way whatever, under pain of excommunication, from which absolution shall not be obtainable through anyone except through Ourselves, or Our Successor, the Roman Pontiff for the time being, unless in the article of death." Benedict XIV (*Providus*, 1751) renewed this condemnation; so did Pius VII (*Ecclesiam*, 1821), who directed censures also against the Italian secret society the Carbonari, and other revolutionary associations. Leo XII (*Quo Graviora*, 1825) also condemned Freemasonry and other secret societies, as did Pius VIII (*Traditae Humilitate*, 1829), Gregory XVI (*Mirari Vos*, 1832), Pius IX (*Qui Pluribus*, 1846; *Singulari Quadam*, 1864, and *Multiplicis*, 1865), and Leo XIII (*Humanum Genus*, 1884). And in the Code of Canon Law (*Codex Juris Canonici*), published in 1917 by Benedict XV, occurs this enactment: " All those who enroll their names in the sect of Freemasons or similar associations plotting against the Church or the legitimate civil authorities incur by the very fact the penalty of excommunication, absolution from which is specially reserved to the Holy See. If the delinquents be clerics or religious [i.e., members of a conventual or other Order under vows], every Catholic is under the obligation of denouncing them to the Congregation of the Holy Office."

We now come to the Encyclicals issued after 1870. We shall confine ourselves almost entirely to those dealing with social and political questions; but at the end of the book will be found summaries of a few which treat of more general theological matters, since they are of interest and importance in general bearing.

LEO XIII, Encyclical *Inscrutabili* (" On the Evils affecting Modern Society "; April 21, 1878): " From the very beginning of Our Pontificate," said the Pope, " the sad sight has presented itself to Us of the evils by which the human race is oppressed on every side. . . . Now, the source of these evils lies chiefly, We are convinced, in this: that the holy and venerable authority of the Church, which in God's name rules mankind, upholding, and defending all lawful authority, has been despised and set aside. . . . If anyone of sound mind compare the age in which we live, so hostile to religion and to the Church of Christ, with those happy times when the Church was revered as a mother by the nations, beyond all question he will see that our epoch is rushing wildly along the straight road to destruction." The Pope declared that the Church is the true promoter of real civilization; that the Holy See must be free and independent (" that We may above all things, and in every possible way, maintain the rights and freedom of the Holy See, We shall never cease to strive that Our authority may meet with due deference; that obstacles may be removed which hamper the free exercise of Our ministry; and that We may be restored to that condition of affairs in which the design of God's wisdom had long ago placed the Roman Pontiffs) " [namely, a measure of independent civil sovereignty]; that philosophy should be the ally of religion;

that God's law should be observed in marriage and the family; and that " the human race, taking warning from so many evils and visitations, should submit themselves at length to the Church, and turn for health and prosperity to the infallible guidance of the Apostolic See."

LEO XIII, Encyclical *Quod Apostolici Muneris* (" Concerning Modern Errors "; December 28, 1878). In this Encyclical the Pope emphatically condemned the revolutionary movements of the time: " You understand as a matter of course, Venerable Brothers, that We are alluding to that sect of men who, under the motley and almost barbarous terms and titles of Socialists, Communists, and Nihilists, are spread abroad throughout the world and, bound intimately together in baneful alliance, no longer look for strong support in secret meetings held in darksome places, but, standing forth openly and boldly in the light of day, strive to carry out the purpose, long resolved upon, of uprooting the foundations of civilized society at large." They attack, said the Pope, authority, the family, and private property. He traced the evil primarily to the Protestant Reformation: " In fact, Venerable Brethren, you know full well that the atrocious war which, starting from the sixteenth century, was declared against the Catholic Faith by the Reformers, and which has been growing amain from day to day in vehemence, aimed at giving free course to the rejection of all revelation, the subversion of the supernatural order, and the enthronement of unaided reason, with its vagaries or rather ravings. . . . It has even been contended that public authority, with its dignity and power of ruling, originates not from God but from the mass of the people, which, considering itself unfettered by all divine sanction, refuses to submit to any laws that it has not itself passed of its own free will." Subjects should be obedient to rulers, but those rulers should govern moderately. If they act tyrannically, " the Sovereign Judge will call them to strict and speedy account." As regards tyrannical rulers, "subjects should not rise against them without further warranty, lest peace and order become more and more disturbed." They should exercise " Christian hope and patience in urgent prayer to God." " But, should it please legislators and rulers to enjoin or sanction anything repugnant to the divine and natural law, then the dignity and duty of the name of Christian, and the Apostolic injunction, proclaim that one *ought to obey God rather than man* (Acts, v, 29)." Marriage is indissoluble. Individuals have the right to hold private property. " It seems expedient to encourage associations for handicraftsmen and working-men, which, placed under the sheltering care of religion, may render the members content with their lot and resigned to toil, inducing them to lead a peaceful and tranquil life."

LEO XIII, Encyclical *Arcanum Divinae* (" On Christian Marriage"; February 10, 1880). The Pope said: " We record what is known to all, and cannot be doubted by any, that God, on the sixth day of creation, having made man from the slime of the earth, and having breathed into his face the breath of life, gave him a companion whom He miraculously took from the side of Adam when he was locked in sleep." From the beginning marriage was meant to possess " unity and perpetuity." It became, however, corrupt amongst the nations. Christ restored it to its first state and made it a Sacrament. The husband is the head of the family: " The husband is the chief of the family, and the head of the wife. The woman, because she is flesh of his flesh and bone of his bone, must be subject to her husband and obey him; not, indeed, as a servant, but as a companion, so that her obedience shall be wanting in neither honour nor dignity." The Church has a right to control Christian marriage: "It ought not to be regulated and administered by the will of civil rulers, but by the Divine authority of the Church." Laws of divorce are a fruitful source of evil: "Matrimonial contracts are by it made variable; mutual kindness is weakened; deplorable inducements to unfaithfulness are supplied; harm is done to the education and training of children; occasion is afforded of the breaking up of homes"; etc. "Mixed marriages" (of Catholics and non-Catholics) are deplored: "They give occasion to forbidden association and communion in religious matters; endanger the faith of the Catholic partner; are a hindrance to the proper education of the children." This Encyclical contains, incidentally, a statement as to the Papal conception of the proper relations of Church and State: "No one doubts that Jesus Christ, the Founder of the Church, willed her sacred power to be distinct from the civil power, and each power to be free and unfettered in its own sphere: with this condition, however—a condition good for both, and of advantage to all men—that union and concord should be maintained between them, and that on those questions which are, though in different ways, of common right and authority, the power to which secular matters have been entrusted should happily and becomingly depend on the other power which has in its charge the interests of heaven." (As to marriage, see also the Encyclical *Casti Connubii* of Pius XI, 1930, summarized later in this book.)

LEO XIII, Encyclical *Immortale Dei* (" On the Christian Constitution of States "; November 1, 1885). "The Catholic Church," says the Pope, " that imperishable handiwork of our all-merciful God, has for her immediate and natural purpose the saving of souls and the securing of happiness in heaven; yet in regard to things temporal she is the source of benefits as manifold and great as if the chief end of her existence were to ensure the prospering of our earthly life." Nevertheless, he goes on, slanders are levelled against the Church as though she were " opposed to the rightful aims of civil government." " We, therefore, deem it of the highest importance to contrast with the lessons taught by Christ the novel theories now advanced concerning the State." God, the Pope declares, is the Author of society and the source of civil authority. " The right to rule, however, is not necessarily bound up with any special mode of government. It may take this or that form, provided only that it is of a nature to ensure the general welfare." " They who rule should do so with even-handed justice, not as masters but rather as fathers." " If those in authority rule unjustly, if they govern over-bearingly or arrogantly, and if their measures prove hurtful to the people, they must remember that the Almighty will one day bring them to account." Yet: " To despise legitimate authority, in whomsoever vested, is unlawful and a rebellion against the Divine Will. . . . To cast aside obedience and by popular violence to incite to revolt, is therefore treason, not against man only, but against God." The State is bound to profess religion: " Since, then, no one is allowed to be remiss in the service due to God, and since the chief duty of all men is to cling to religion in both its teaching and practice—not such a religion as they may prefer, but the religion which God enjoins, and which most clear and sure marks show to be the alone true religion— . . . it is a sin for the State not to have a care for religion, as a something beyond its scope, or of no practical benefit; or out of many forms of religion to adopt that one which chimes in with the fancy—for we are bound absolutely to worship God in the way which He has shown to be His will." " Just as the end at which the Church aims is by far the noblest of ends, so is its authority the most exalted of all authority, nor can it be looked upon as inferior to the civil power, or in any manner dependent upon it." The Church must have its independent power as "a perfect society": "In very truth Jesus Christ gave to His Apostles unrestrained authority in sacred matters, together with the genuine and most true power of making laws, as also with the duplex right of judging and punishing, which flow from that power." "The Almighty has appointed the charge of the human race between two powers, the ecclesiastical and the civil, the one being set over divine, the other over human things. Each in its kind is supreme, each has fixed limits." They should work in agreement. Sad to say, however, "since the harmful rage for innovation which rose to a climax in the sixteenth century," discord has arisen. The State even has come "to believe that it is not obliged to make profession of any religion; or to enquire which of the many religions is the only true one; or to prefer one religion to all the rest, or to show to any form of religion any special favour; but, on the contrary [the State has come to think that], it is bound to grant equal rights to every creed." As a result of this, says the Pope, we have unrestrained liberty by which "everyone has boundless licence to think whatever he chooses and to publish abroad whatever he thinks. Now, when the State rests on bases like these, it readily appears into what and how unrightful a position the Church is driven. For when the management of public business is in harmony with doctrines of such a kind, the Catholic religion is allowed a standing in civil society equal only, or inferior, to societies alien from it; no regard is paid to the laws of the Church, and she who, by the order and commission of Jesus Christ, has the duty of teaching all nations, finds herself forbidden to take part in the instruction of the people." "So too," continues the Pope, "the liberty of thinking and publishing whatsoever each one likes, without let or hindrance, is not in itself an advantage over which society can wisely rejoice. On the contrary, it is the fount and origin of many evils. Liberty is a power perfecting man, and hence should have truth and goodness for its object." The Church therefore condemns separation of Church and State and " the unrestrained liberty of thinking and openly making known one's thoughts," and insists on the duty of the civil power to work in harmony with the ecclesiastical. " The sovereignty of the people, and this without any reference to God, is held to reside in the multitude—which is doubtless a doctrine exceedingly well calculated to flatter and enflame many passions, but which lacks all proof by reason." Yet: " It is not blameworthy in itself, in any manner, for the people to have a share, greater or less, in the government: for at certain times, and under certain laws, such participation may not only be of benefit to the citizens, but may even be of obligation." As to toleration: " The Church indeed deems it unlawful to place various forms of Divine Worship on the same footing as the true religion; but she does not, on that account, condemn those rulers who, for the sake of securing some great good, or of hindering some great evil, tolerate in practice that these various forms of religion have a place in the State."

LEO XIII, Encyclical *Libertas Praestantissimum Donum* (" On Human Liberty "; June 20, 1888). " Liberty, the highest of all natural endowments, being the portion only of intellectual and rational natures, confers on man this dignity—that he is *in the hand of his counsel* and has power over his actions." Man is free to follow good or to turn aside to evil. In the right use of freedom man has the support of the Church. " Yet there are many who imagine that the Church is hostile to human liberty. Having a false and absurd notion of what liberty is, either they pervert the very idea of freedom, or they extend it at their pleasure to many things in respect of which man cannot rightly be regarded as free." "The end, or object, both of the rational will and of its liberty, is that good which is in conformity with reason." When the will chooses evil, it acts defectively. The will has need of law, and its guide should be the law of God. Human law should be based on Divine Law. Of that Law the Catholic Church is the exponent. That modern Liberalism, which would give freedom to all opinion, leads to irrational and harmful consequences. The civil State is amenable to the Law of God. "Let us," goes on the Pope, "examine that liberty in individuals which is so opposed to the virtue of religion, namely, the *liberty of worship*, as it is called. This is based on the principle that every man is free to profess, as he may choose, any religion or none. . . . This kind of liberty, if considered in relation to the State, clearly implies that there is no reason why the State should offer any homage to God, or should desire any public recognition of Him; that no one form of religion should be preferred to another, but that all stand on equal footing. . . . [But] Justice therefore forbids, and reason itself forbids, the State to be godless—or to adopt a line of action which would end in godlessness: namely, to treat the various religions (as they call them) alike, and to bestow upon them promiscuously equal rights and privileges. Since, then, the profession of one religion is necessary in the State, that religion must be professed which alone is true, and which can be recognized without difficulty, especially in Catholic States, because the marks of truth are, as it were, engraven upon it." As to "liberty of speech," "liberty of the Press," and "liberty of teaching," these are evil unless guided by the Law of God as taught by the Church: for "the liberty of which We have been speaking is greatly opposed to reason, and tends absolutely to pervert men's minds, inasmuch as it claims for itself the right of teaching whatever it pleases—a liberty which the State cannot grant without failing in its duty." The Church substitutes, for the false, a true idea of freedom: " It is of no small advantage for the perfecting of human liberty: since our Saviour Jesus Christ said that by truth is man made free: *You shall know the truth, and truth shall make you free* (John, viii, 32). Therefore there is no reason why genuine liberty should grow indignant, or true science feel aggrieved, at having to bear the just and necessary restraint of laws, by which, in the judgment of the Church and of reason itself, human teaching has to be controlled." Still, as a measure of expedience, toleration of error may be at times needful: " With the discernment of a true Mother, the Church weighs the great burden of human weakness, and well knows the course down which the minds and actions of man are in this our age being borne. For this reason, while not conceding any right to anything save what is true and honest, she does not forbid public authority to tolerate what is at variance with truth and justice, for the sake of avoiding some greater evil, or of obtaining or preserving some greater good. . . . But, to judge aright, we must acknowledge that the more a State is driven to tolerate evil the further it is from perfection; and that the tolerance of evil which is dictated by political prudence should be confined strictly to the limits which its justifying cause—the public welfare— demands. . . . And although in the extraordinary con- dition of these times the Church usually acquiesces in certain modern liberties—not because she prefers them in them- selves, but because she judges it expedient to permit them— she would in happier times exercise her own liberty, and, by persuasion, exhortation, and entreaty, would endeavour, as she is bound, to fulfil the duty assigned to her by God of providing for the eternal salvation of mankind. . . .

[Some people] oppose not the existence of the Church—
nor, indeed, could they; yet they despoil her of the nature
and rights of a perfect society, and maintain that it does not
belong to her to legislate, to judge, and to punish, but only
to exhort, to advise, and to rule her subjects in accordance
with their own consent and will.   By such opinion they
pervert the nature of this divine society, and attenuate and
narrow its authority, its office of teacher, and its whole
efficiency."   The Church nevertheless does not condemn
all forms of modern Liberalism: " To reject the supreme
authority of God, and to cast off all obedience to Him in
public matters or even in private and domestic affairs, is the
greatest perversion of liberty and the worst kind of Liberalism: and what We have said must be understood to apply
to this alone, in its fullest sense."   As to democracy:
" It is not in itself wrong to prefer a democratic form of
government, if only the Catholic doctrine be maintained as
to the origin and exercise of power.   Of the various forms
of government, the Church does not reject any that are
fitted to secure the welfare of the subject—that they should
be constituted without involving wrong to anyone, and
especially without violating the rights of the Church."

LEO XIII, Encyclical *Sapientiae Christianae* (" On the
Chief Duties of Christians as Citizens "; January 10, 1890).
" From day to day it becomes more and more evident,"
said the Pope, at the beginning of this Letter, " how needful
it is that the principles of Christian Wisdom should be
borne always in mind, and that the life, the morals, and the
institutions of nations should be wholly conformed to them.
From the fact of these principles having been disregarded,
mischiefs so vast have accrued, that no right-minded man
can face the trials of the time without grave solicitude, nor
contemplate the future without serious harm."   " If," he
continues, " a civil government strives after external

advantages merely, and the attainment of such objects as
adorn life; if in administering public affairs it is wont to
put God aside, and shows no care in upholding the moral
law—then it deflects woefully from its right course and
from the injunctions of nature: nor should such a gathering-
together and association of men be accounted as a common-
wealth, but only as a deceitful imitation and make-believe of
civil organisation." Nations and individuals must return
to religion. The Church favours true patriotism: " The
supernatural love for the Church, and the natural love of
our own country, proceed from the same eternal principle,
since God Himself is their author and originating Cause."
" Law is of its very essence a mandate of right reason,
proclaimed by a properly constituted authority, for the
common good. But a true and legitimate authority is void
of sanction unless it proceed from God, the supreme Ruler
and Lord of all." " If the laws of the State are manifestly
at variance with the Divine Law, containing enactments
hurtful to the Church, or conveying injunctions adverse to
the duties imposed by religion, or if they violate in the
person of the Supreme Pontiff the authority of Jesus Christ,
then, truly, to resist becomes a positive duty, to obey, a
crime: a crime moreover combined with misdemeanour
against the State itself, inasmuch as every offence levelled
against religion is also a sin against the State. Here anew
it becomes evident how unjust is the reproach of sedition:
for the obedience due to lawgivers is not refused, but there
is a deviation from their will in those precepts only which
they have no power to enjoin. Commands that are issued
adversely to the honour due to God, and hence are beyond
the scope of justice, must be looked upon as anything
rather than laws." Catholics must always be ready to
defend the Faith and, in so doing, to act in common: " To
bring about such a union of minds and uniformity of action

—not without reason so feared by the enemies of Catholicism—the main point is that a perfect harmony of opinion should prevail." "Union of minds, therefore, requires, together with a perfect accord in the one Faith, complete submission and obedience of will to the Church and to the Roman Pontiff, as to God Himself." "This likewise must be reckoned amongst the duties of Christians, that they allow themselves to be ruled and directed by the rulership and leadership of bishops, and, above all, of the Apostolic See." "Since the Church is not only a perfect society in herself, but is superior to every other society of human growth, she refuses resolutely—prompted alike by right and by duty—to link herself to any mere party and to subject herself to the fleeting exigencies of politics. . . . It is not her province to decide which is the best amongst many diverse forms of government and the civil institutions of Christian States, and amid the various kinds of State rule she does not disapprove of any, provided the respect due to religion, and the observance of good morals, be upheld." "It does not hence follow, however, that Church and State are in any manner severed, and, still less, antagonistic." "From God has been the duty assigned to the Church, not only to interpose resistance, if at any time the State rule should run counter to religion, but further to make a strong endeavour that the power of the Gospel may pervade the laws and institutions of the nations."

LEO XIII, Encyclical *Rerum Novarum* (" On the Condition of the Working Classes "; May 15, 1891). This is regarded by Catholics as one of the most notable if not *the* most notable of this Pope's Encyclicals. A prominent English Catholic writer, the Rev. Henry Parkinson (Preface to the 1912 edition of the Catholic Truth Society volume, *The Pope and the People : Select Encyclicals of Leo XIII*), said of it: " The appearance of the *Rerum Novarum* had been preceded by the studies and energetic propaganda of Bishop Ketteler and Baron Volgesang in Germany, Gaspard Decurtins in Switzerland, T. Funck-Bretano, the Marquis de la Tour-du-Pin and the Comte de Mun in France, and Liberatore in Italy. Still, the great ' Charter of the Workman,' as it has been justly called, came at a time when the world was unripe for its Gospel teaching. Perhaps it was part of its providential mission to hasten the ripening. It was received at first with apathy and reluctance in some quarters, and was certainly slow in its effect upon society; but its triumph is now assured, though its conquest is not yet complete. It is much more than a letter on social and economic subjects; it is the opening out of the economic system of the Church in human society." Leo began by denouncing the evils of " the enormous fortunes of some individuals, and the utter poverty of the masses." " By degrees it has come to pass, " he said, " that working-men have been surrendered, isolated and helpless, to the hardheartedness of employers and the greed of unchecked competition." " To remedy these wrongs the Socialists, working on the poor man's envy of the rich, are striving to do away with private property, and they contend that individual possessions should become the common property of all, to be administered by the State or by municipal bodies." By that theory, however, " they would rob the lawful possessor, distort the functions of the State, and create utter confusion in the community." The working-man himself would suffer: " Socialists, therefore, by trying to transfer the possessions of individuals to the community at large, strike at the interests of every wage-earner, since they would deprive him of the liberty of disposing of his wages, and thereby of all hope and possibility of increasing his resources and of bettering his condition in life." Ownership of private property (including land) is a natural right:

c

" When man turns the activity of his mind, and the strength of his body, towards procuring the fruits of nature, by such act he makes his own that portion of nature's field which he cultivates—that portion on which he leaves, as it were, the impress of his individuality; and it cannot but be just that he should possess that portion as his very own." Excessive State interference is mischievous: " Not only is such interference unjust, but it is quite certain to harass and worry all classes of citizens, and subject them to odious and intolerable bondage." Society should not be " class-less ": " It is impossible to reduce human society to one dead level. . . . People differ in capacity, skill, health, strength; and unequal fortune is a necessary result of unequal condition." " It is a great mistake to take up with the notion that class is naturally hostile to class, and that the wealthy and the working-men are intended by nature to live in mutual conflict. So irrational is this view, and so false, that the direct contrary is the truth. . . . In a State it is ordained by nature that these two classes should dwell in harmony and agreement, so as to maintain the balance of the body politic. Each needs the other. Capital cannot do without Labour, nor Labour without Capital." The workers must have adequate wages: " Doubtless, before deciding whether wages are fair, many things have to be considered: but wealthy owners, and all masters of labour, should be mindful of this—that to exercise pressure upon the indigent and the destitute, for the sake of gain, and to gather one's profit out of the need of another, is condemned by all laws human and divine." The wealthy have the duty to be charitable: " When what necessity demands has been supplied, and one's standing fairly taken thought of, it becomes a duty to give to the indigent out of what remains over. *Of that which remaineth, give alms* (Luke, xi, 41.)." As regards conditions of work: " It is neither just nor humane so to grind men down by excessive labour as to stupefy their minds and wear out their bodies." "Women, again, are not suited for certain occupations; a woman by nature is fitted for home-work." The wages of the working-man should not be regulated by free contract only, and "ought not to be insufficient to support a frugal and well-conducted wage-earner. If, through necessity or fear of a worse evil, the workman accept harder conditions because an employer or contractor will afford him no better, he is made the victim of force and injustice." "If a workman's wages be sufficient to enable him comfortably to support himself, his wife, and his children, he will find it easy, if he be a sensible man, to practise thrift; and he will not fail, by reducing expenses, to put by some little savings and thus secure a modest source of income. . . . The law should favour ownership, and its policy should be to induce as many as possible of the people to become owners." The Pope favoured Trade Unions: "History attests what excellent results were brought about by the Artificers' Guilds of olden times. . . . It is a natural impulse which binds men together in civil society; and it is likewise that which leads them to join in associations which, though lesser and not independent societies, are, nevertheless, societies." "There is a good deal of evidence, however, which goes to prove that many of these societies are in the hands of secret leaders, and are managed on principles ill-according with Christianity and the public benefit"; therefore the Pope inclines to favour separate Catholic Trade Unions: "Under those circumstances Christian working-men must do one of two things—either join associations in which their religion will be exposed to peril, or form others among themselves: unite their forces and courageously shake off the yoke of so unjust and unbearable an aggression. No one who does not wish to expose man's chief good to extreme risk will for a moment hesitate to say that the second alternative should by all means be adopted." (As to the Encyclical *Quadragesimo Anno*, by which Pope Pius XI, in 1931, confirmed and commemorated *Rerum Novarum*, see later in this book.)

LEO XIII, Encyclical *Graves de Communi* (" On Christian Democracy"; January 18, 1901). " Through the harmful influence of agitators," began this Encyclical, " the gulf between rich and poor has been widened, so that frequent disturbances arise and even great calamities seem impending." The Pope aims, therefore, at " maintaining the claims of justice and religion, and removing all occasion of strife between classes." " What ' Social Democracy ' means, and what ' Christian Democracy ' ought to mean, surely admits of no doubt. . . . The former wishes to place the supreme power in the hands of the masses, so that, having abolished distinctions of classes, they may proceed to an equal distribution of wealth; and so the right to own private property is to be done away with. . . . But ' Christian Democracy,' as Christian, . . . must insist that ' the right to have and to hold ' be kept inviolate; it must maintain the distinction between classes, which belongs properly to a well-ordered State." The " social question " is first of all moral and religious: " That is why We have never encouraged Catholics to form associations to better the lot of the working class, or introduce other schemes of the kind, without at the same time warning them that such things must not be attempted without the sanction of religion." The Pope encourages alms-giving: " No doubt Socialists carp at this, and would have it altogether abolished, as derogatory to the native nobility of man. Yet if it is done according to the precepts of the Gospel and in a Christian manner, it neither feeds the pride of the giver nor inflicts any humiliation on the recipient. . . . It rather fosters the friendliness of mutual service."

PIUS X (immediate successor of Leo XIII), Motu Proprio *Fin dalla Prima* (" On Christian Social Action "; December 18, 1903). " We who," said the then newly-elected Pope, " no less than Our predecessor, recognizing how needful it is to guide Christian popular action rightly, desire that those most prudent rules [that were laid down by Leo XIII] should be exactly and fully observed, and that no one should be so bold as to set them aside." Therefore, the Pope " collects them into the following articles." These are: (1) Men are not equal in everything; (2) Their equality is in that all were created by God, redeemed by Christ, and will be judged by God; (3) Inequality of " princes and subjects, masters and men, rich and poor, learned and ignorant, nobles and plebeians," is natural; (4–5) Private property is a right; (6) There is a distinction between justice and charity: " Only when justice has been violated is there a right to make a claim "; (7) " The obligations of the poor and of the workman are: To perform wholly and with fidelity the work freely and equitably agreed upon; not to injure masters in their goods or persons; to abstain from acts of violence, even in defence of their own rights, and never to turn their demands into disturbances "; (8) " The obligations of justice for capitalists and masters are: To pay a just wage to workmen; not to injure their lawful savings by violence, fraud, nor by open or hidden usury; to allow them freely to fulfil their religious duties; not to expose them to corrupting allurements, nor to the danger of scandal; not to entice them from a love of their family, and from careful thrift; not to impose on them work unsuited to their strength, age, and sex "; (9) The rich have a duty " to help the poor and needy "; (10) Poverty is not a thing of which to be ashamed; (11) Capitalists and workmen should form associations mutually helpful; (12) " Christian " is different from " Social Democracy," since the former " is based on the principles of Catholic faith and morality, especially on that of never attacking in any way the inviolable right of private property "; (13) Christian Democracy must not tie itself to any political party (especially in Italy " under existing circumstances, for reasons of the highest order) " [this, of course, was before the 1929 restoration of a measure of Papal temporal rule]; (14) Christian Democracy must be subject to ecclesiastical control; (15) In Italy it must be controlled by " the Catholic Congresses and Committees " under the bishops; (16) Catholic writers must be guided by the Pope and bishops; (17) They must be subject to censorship of " all writings relating to religion, Christian morality, and natural ethics." " Clerics ought also to obtain permission of the Ordinary [bishop] previous to the publication of writings even of a technical character "; (18) In all writings " charity and harmony " should be observed, " avoiding all abusive language and reproaches "; (19) There must be no stirring up of class hatred.

Pius X, Encyclical *Il Fermo Proposito* (" On Christian Social Action "; June 11, 1905). " Immense is the field of Catholic action; it excludes absolutely nothing which in any manner, directly or indirectly, belongs to the divine mission of the Church." " *To restore all things in Christ* has ever been the Church's motto, and it is especially Ours, in the perilous times in which we live." " The Church, throughout her long history, has always and on every occasion luminously shown that she possesses a wonderful power of adaptation to the varying conditions of human society; without injury to the integrity and immutability of faith and morals, she easily bends and adapts herself in all that is contingent and accidental, and to the fresh needs of society." Catholics must bestir themselves, under ecclesiastical guidance, " by the efficacious propaganda of the

Press, by the living exhortation of speech, . . . to ameliorate, within the limits of justice and charity, the economic condition of the people, supporting and promoting those institutions which conduce to this end, and those especially which aim at fortifying the multitude against the invasion of Socialism."

BENEDICT XV (immediate successor of Pius X), Encyclical *Ad Beatissimi* (" On the Outbreak of the European War "; November 1, 1914). " On every side the dread phantom of war holds sway; there is scarce room for another thought in the minds of men. . . . Who would recognize brothers whose Father is in heaven? . . . We implore Kings and Rulers to consider the floods of tears and blood already poured out, and to hasten to restore to the nations the blessings of peace." " Ever since the precepts and practices of Christian Wisdom ceased to be observed in the ruling of States, it followed that, as they contained the peace and stability of institutions, the very foundations of States necessarily began to be shaken. Such, moreover, has been the change in the ideas and morals of Men, that, unless God comes soon to our help, the end of civilization would seem to be at hand." " Race hatred has reached its climax; peoples are more divided by jealousies than by frontiers; within one and the same nation, within the same city, there rages the burning envy of class against class; and amongst individuals it is self-love which is the supreme law over-riding everything." " *There is no power but from God; and those that are, are ordained of God* (Rom., xiii, 1). . . . Let the princes and rulers of peoples remember this truth, and let them consider whether it is a prudent and safe idea for Governments or States to separate themselves from the holy religion of Jesus Christ." " The errors of Socialism, and similar doctrines," should be resisted.

THE PAPAL PEACE PROPOSALS. On August 1, 1917,

Pope Benedict XV, after " the first world-war " had lasted three years, addressed, by diplomatic channels " to the heads of the belligerent peoples," a document (*Dès le Début*) making suggestions " for a just and lasting peace." " First," he said, " the fundamental point should be that the moral force of right should replace the material force of arms." There should be " a simultaneous and reciprocal agreement for the diminution of armaments "; " then, in the place of armaments, the establishment of arbitration "; there should be " true freedom and common enjoyment of the seas "; " complete and reciprocal condonation " of all war-damages; evacuation of occupied territories; and fair settlement of territorial questions. The proposals met with no acceptance, and the war continued for more than another year. A Catholic comment, written sixteen years afterwards (London *Catholic Times*, December 8, 1933, article on " Vatican Diplomacy "), said: " The failure of his Peace Note in 1917 seemed to the Allies in November, 1918, to be a blessing. But does the world to-day think that a negotiated peace in 1917, on the lines of the Papal suggestion, would be worse than the dictated peace of Versailles? . . . Some failures are glorious, and Pope Benedict's was one." That is a problem for historians. On May 23, 1920, Pope Benedict issued an Encyclical (*Pacem Dei Munus Pulcherrimum :* " On the Re-establishment of Christian Peace ") calling on nations and individuals " to forget mutual differences and offences and draw together in the bonds of Christian charity."

Pius XI, Encyclical *Ubi Arcano Dei* (" On the Troubles left by the European War "; December 23, 1922). Pius XI, who succeeded Benedict on the latter's death, devoted his first Encyclical to the woes left by the war. The first of the evils he deplored was " that ' class-war ' which has penetrated among the nations like a deadly infection, poisoning work, the arts, commerce, everything, in fact, that tends to public and private well-being." " Thence come frequent strikes and lock-outs, public disturbance and repression, damage and discontent for all." Family life also has become dislocated. There is decay of religion: " widespread neglect of Christian duties." " Peace indeed was signed between the belligerents, but it was written in public documents, not in the hearts of men." " But there is a Divine Institution able to safeguard the sanctity of the law of nations: an institution both belonging to and at the same time superior to all nations—endowed with the highest authority and venerable for the perfection of its teaching office. . . . In human society, rightly con- stituted, the Church, carrying out her divine mission, could uphold those principles and commands of God Himself among individuals and society as a whole." The Pope gave a tentative hint at a possibility of re-assembling the Vatican Ecumenical Council (which had dispersed in 1870 without being formally concluded), but he " did not go so far as directly to include it in Our programme. . . . Like the illustrious leader of the Israelites [see Judges, vi, 17], We must wait, praying the while that the Lord may grant Us clearer indication of His will." In the event, the Council was not re-assembled. The Pope also expressed a desire for reconciliation with Italy, the dispute over the Papal Temporal power being then still unsettled: " Italy will never have to fear hurt from the Holy See. . . . It will be for the Almighty and Merciful God to bring about that this most blessed day [of reconciliation] shall dawn at last."

[For Encyclical *Quas Primas*, 1925, " On the Feast of Christ the King," see page 95.]

THE LATERAN TREATY

Pope Pius had not long to wait for " the dawn of this most blessed day." On February 11, 1929, he addressed the parish priests of Rome, and, after dealing with general matters, said: " And now we come to that other matter which makes your presence and your help more than ever dear and welcome to Us, and which will render this gathering memorable and historical, independently of the fact that We are celebrating the seventh anniversary of Our Coronation and the year of Our priestly Jubilee. On this very day, at this very hour, quite possibly at this very moment, yonder in Our palace of the Lateran a Treaty and a Concordat are being signed by His Eminence, the Secretary of State, as Our plenipotentiary, and by Cavaliere Benito Mussolini, as plenipotentiary of H.M. the King of Italy: A Treaty which recognizes, and, as far as human powers go, assures to the Holy See a true, proper, and real territorial sovereignty. . . . A Concordat, moreover, which from the first We have willed to be indissolubly connected with the Treaty, and which is framed to regulate duly the religious state of Italy, outraged by a series of governments, either themselves sectarian, or leagued in obedience to the enemies of the Church, though in some cases not individually hostile." The Pope continued: " The Vicar of Jesus Christ is not influenced by worldly greed, but only by the recognition of that which it is impossible not to ask for: because a territorial sovereignty of this sort is universally recognized as an indispensable condition for all real sovereignty of jurisdiction. Accordingly, a minimum of territory, just enough for the exercise of sovereignty: as much territory as is necessary for its actual subsistence, as otherwise it will have no support." In point of fact (to quote an anonymous Catholic writer: *How the " Roman Question " was Settled*; London Catholic Truth Society, August, 1936; p. 12, footnote): " The States of the Church, as they existed prior to 1860, comprised 15,774 square miles and 3,000,000 inhabitants: the ' City of the Vatican ' will be probably less than one square mile in extent." Three days after this speech, the Pope addressed a delegation from Milan University, and emphasized the importance he attached to the Concordat which accompanied the Treaty: " It is in the Concordat that the Treaty finds not only its explanation, not only its justification, but its recommendation as well." The Concordat designated Catholicism as the religion of Italy; recognized marriage as indissoluble; enforced religious teaching in schools; and, amongst other provisions, declared that priests who may have left the Church could not be employed as teachers or in Government service. Italy also " recognizes the Catholic organizations forming part of ' the Italian Catholic Action,' which, according to the instructions of the Holy See, must keep their activities outside any political party and under the immediate control of the hierarchy of the Church for the purpose of spreading and applying Catholic principles." " The financial convention establishes that the Holy See— as a definitive settlement of all its financial relations with Italy in consequence of the fall of its temporal power— accepts 750,000,000 lire cash [£8,300,000] and 1,000,000,000 lire [£11,000,000] in Italian State bonds bearing interest at 5 per cent." In the speech to the Milan delegation the Pope said: " We may say We were most generously helped by the other side. It may be that there was also needed a man such as Providence has caused Us to meet, a man unaffected by the prejudices of the ' Liberal School ' [Mussolini], . . . and thus, with the Grace of God, with much patience and much labour, thanks to constant and generous assistance, We have succeeded, *per medium pro-*

fundum, in drawing up a Concordat which, if not actually *the* very best possible, is certainly to be reckoned among the best."

We may now return to our summaries of Papal Encyclicals:—

PIUS XI (Encyclical *Rappresentanti in Terra*: " On the Christian Education of Youth "; December 31, 1929). " Since," says the Pope, " education consists essentially in preparing man for what he must be and for what he must do here below, in order to attain the sublime end for which he was created, it is clear that there can be no true education which is not wholly directed to man's last end, and that in the present order of Providence, since God has revealed Himself in the person of His Only Begotten Son, who alone is ' the way, the truth, and the life,' there can be no ideally perfect education which is not Christian education." Education is a matter for " three necessary societies, distinct from one another and yet harmoniously combined by God, into which man is born: two, namely, the family and civil society, belong to the natural order; the third, the Church, to the supernatural order." " And first of all education belongs pre-eminently to the Church, by reason of a double title in the supernatural order, conferred exclusively upon her by God Himself; absolutely superior therefore to any other title in the natural order." " It is the inalienable right, as well as the indispensable duty, of the Church to watch over the entire education of her children in all institutions, public or private, not merely in regard to the religious instruction there given, but in regard to every other branch of learning and every regulation in so far as religion and morality are concerned. (*Code of Canon Law,* cc. 1381, 1382) ". " The extent of the Church's mission in the field of education is such as to include every nation, without exception, according to the command of Christ: ' Teach ye all nations ' (Matt: xxviii, 19: *docete omnes gentes*); and there is no power on earth that may lawfully oppose her or stand in her way." Under Church guidance the family should be supreme, and anterior to the power of the State: " The family therefore holds directly from the Creator the mission and hence the right to educate the offspring: a right inalienable because inseparably joined to the strict obligation, a right anterior to any right whatever of civil society and of the State, and therefore inviolable on the part of any power on earth." " On this point the common sense of mankind is in such complete accord, that they would be in open contradiction with it who dared maintain that the children belong to the State before they belong to the family, and that the State has absolute right over their education." " So jealous is she [the Church] of the family's inviolable natural right to educate the children, that she never consents, save under peculiar circumstances and with special cautions, to baptize the children of unbelievers, or provide for their education against the will of the parents, till such time as the children can choose for themselves and freely embrace the Faith (*Code of Canon Law*, c. 750, §2)." " Accordingly, in the matter of education, it is the right, or, to speak more directly, it is the duty, of the State to protect, in its legislation, the prior rights, already described, of the family as regards the Christian education of its offspring, and consequently also to respect the supernatural rights of the Church in this same realm of Christian education." " The so-called ' neutral,' or ' lay,' school—from which religion is excluded—is contrary to the fundamental principles of education. Such a school, moreover, cannot exist in practice; it is bound to become irreligious." Catholics must insist on having their own schools, in which " all the teaching, and the whole organization, and its teachers, syllabus, and text-books in every branch, be regulated by the Christian spirit, under the direction and maternal supervision of the Church."

THE POPE AND RUSSIA. The London *Catholic Herald* (January 10, 1932; article, " What the Holy See Fears ": " from a Correspondent in Rome ") wrote thus : " I believe [that], when the history of his pontificate comes to be written, it will be found that the Russian army at the gates of Warsaw, when Pope Pius XI was nuncio [Papal ambassador] there just after the [1914–1918] Great War, has exercised a tremendous influence on his mind. It explains his attitude to the Nazi government in Germany : *anything better than atheistic Communism*. He has witnessed during his pontificate the Communist risings in Spain and Brazil; he has seen Italy and Germany on the verge of it. He knows its strength in France." Pius XI's attitude to Soviet Russia fully confirms this statement. On February 2, 1930 (two years before the appearance of the *Catholic Herald's* article), he had addressed to Cardinal Pompili, Bishop of Velletri and Papal Vicar-general in Rome, a letter on " The Soviet Campaign against God." " We are," he said, " deeply moved by the horrible and sacrilegious crimes that are repeated every day against God and against the vast population of Russia." " From the very beginning of Our Pontificate," he continued, " following the example of Our Predecessor of holy memory, Benedict XV, We multiplied Our efforts to put an end to this terrible persecution and to avert the grievous evils that press upon these people. We were also at pains to ask the Governments represented at the Conference of Genoa, to make, by common agreement, a declaration which might have saved Russia and all the world from many woes, demanding, as a condition preliminary to any recognition of the Soviet

Government, respect for conscience, freedom of worship and of church property. Alas, these three points, so essential above all to those ecclesiastical hierarchies unhappily separated from Catholic unity [the Russian Orthodox Church], were abandoned in favour of temporal interests." The Pope described his efforts to bring aid to starving Russians; and went on: "But the fresh outbreak of blasphemies and sacrileges, now officially published, demands a still more solemn and universal reparation. During the feast of last Christmas, not only were many hundreds of churches closed, numerous ikons [sacred pictures] burned, all the workers forced to work, the children compelled to attend school, and the Sundays suppressed; but things have come to such a pass that those employed in the workshops, both men and women, are forced to sign a declaration of formal apostasy and hatred of God, under pain of being deprived of their tickets for food, clothing, and lodging, without which every inhabitant of that unhappy country must die of hunger, distress, and cold. Moreoever, there were organized in all towns and many villages infamous carnival pageants similar to those which the foreign diplomats beheld last Christmas in Moscow itself, in the very centre of their capital. Lorries were seen going by, on which were numbers of youths, dressed in sacred vestments, holding crosses upon which they spat. On other lorries were erected large Christmas trees, on which numerous dolls, dressed to represent Catholic and Orthodox bishops, were hanged by the neck. Then, in the middle of the city, other youths performed acts of sacrilege of every kind against the Cross." As a religious reparation, the Pope ordered special prayers to be offered up, in all Catholic churches, for Russia, and attached to them these Indulgences " 300 days to all who recite either [of the prayers prescribed] with devotion; Plenary, on the usual conditions, to all who recite either prayer every day, during a month." (As to the Pope's Encyclical, *Divini Redemptoris*, " On Atheist Communism ": 1937, see later in this book.)

PIUS XI, Encyclical *Casti Connubii* (" On Christian Marriage "; December 31, 1930). This Letter followed the lines, and supplemented the teachings, of the Encyclical *Arcanum Divinae*, issued by Leo XIII in 1880 (see earlier in this book). " How great," began the Pope, " is the dignity of chaste wedlock, Venerable Brethren, can be judged best from this, that Christ our Lord, Son of the Eternal Father, having assumed the nature of fallen man, not only, with His loving desire of compassing the redemption of our race, ordained it in an especial manner as the principle and foundation of domestic society and therefore of all human intercourse, but also raised it to a true and great Sacrament of the New Law, restored it to the original purity of its divine institution, and accordingly entrusted all its discipline and care to His spouse the Church." Later he said: " Hence these laws [divine] cannot be subject to any human decrees or to any contrary pact even of the spouses themselves." " This union includes both the primacy of the husband with regard to the wife and children, and the ready subjection of the wife and her willing obedience." " This subjection, however, does not deny or take away the liberty which belongs in full to the woman both in view of her dignity as a human person, and in view of her most noble office as wife and mother and companion." No power " can ever affect for any cause whatsoever a Christian marriage which is valid and has been consummated—for as it is plain that here the marriage contract has its full completion, so by the will of God there is also the greatest firmness and indissolubility which may not be destroyed by any human authority." The Pope emphatically condemns " artificial birth-control ": " Since, therefore, the conjugal act is destined primarily by nature for the begetting of children, those who in exercising it frustrate deliberately its natural power and purpose, sin against nature and commit a deed shameful and vicious in itself. . . . The Catholic Church, to whom God has entrusted the defence of the integrity and purity of morals, standing erect in the midst of the moral ruin around her, in order that she may preserve the chastity of the nuptial union from being defiled by this foul stain, raises her voice in token of her divine ambassadorship and through Our mouth proclaims anew: Any use whatsoever of matrimony exercised in such a way that the act is deliberately frustrated of its natural power to generate life, is an offence against the law of God, and those who indulge in such are branded with the guilt of a grave sin." This not only is remarkably outspoken in itself, but the particular passage of the Encyclical has all the appearance of being such as to comply with the 1870 Vatican Council's definition of Papal Infallibility. The Pope in the Encyclical earlier had condemned some modern theories as to " temporary," " experimental," and " companionate " marriages. [Those who advocate these] " do not seem even to suspect that these proposals partake of nothing of the modern ' culture ' in which they glory so much, but are simply odious atrocities which beyond all question reduce our truly cultured nations to the barbarous standards of savage peoples." Then, after the condemnation of " birth-control," he censured proposals for " eugenic reforms," such as " sterilizing the unfit." As to " the unfit," he said: " Although often these persons are to be dissuaded from entering into matrimony, certainly it is wrong to brand men with the stigma of crime because they contract marriage. . . . Public magistrates have no direct power over the bodies of their subjects; therefore, where no crime has taken place and there is no cause present for grave

D

punishment, they can never directly harm, or tamper with, the integrity of the body, either for the reason of eugenics or for any other reason." Towards the end of the Encyclical the Pope quoted and re-affirmed the statement, concerning " Church and State," which occurred in Leo XIII's *Arcanum Divinae*.

PIUS XI, Encyclical *Quadragesimo Anno* (" On the Reconstruction of the Social Order "; May 15, 1931). This long and elaborate Letter was in commemoration of Leo XIII's *Rerum Novarum* (see earlier in this book). It confirmed amply, and supplemented, that Encyclical, and named (also confirming) others of Leo's: especially *Arcanum Divinae*, *Immortale Dei*, *Sapientiae Christianae*, *Quod Apostolici Muneris*, and *Libertas Praestantissimum Donum*. Pope Pius began: " Forty years have elapsed since the incomparable Encyclical of Leo XIII of happy memory, *Rerum Novarum*, first saw the light. The whole Catholic world gratefully recalls the event, and prepares to celebrate it with befitting solemnity." " The Encyclical *Rerum Novarum*," continued the Pope, " completely overthrew those tottering tenets of Liberalism which had long hampered effective interference by the Government." Pope Pius commended Trade Unions, especially if Catholic: " The directions authoritatively promulgated by Leo XIII . . . have a high distinction—that of encouraging Christian workmen to form unions according to their various trades, and of teaching them how to do it." " It must be set to the credit of the Encyclical that these unions of workmen have everywhere so flourished in our days, though unfortunately still inferior in number to the unions of Socialists and of Communists." The Pope reiterates the Church's claim to a voice in politics and sociology: " Our weighty office of declaring, interpreting, and urging, in and out of season, the entire moral law, demands that both the social order and

economic life be brought within Our supreme jurisdiction."
He defends the right of private property, but (" since there
are some who falsely and unjustly accuse the Supreme
Pontiff and the Church of upholding the wealthier classes
against the proletariat ") he disclaims supporting abuses of
that right. "It follows from the duplex character of
ownership—which, as We have said, is both individual and
social—that men must take into account in this matter, not
only their own advantage, but the common good. To
define in detail these duties, when the need occurs, and when
the natural law does not do so, is the function of the civil
ruler. Provided that the natural and divine law be observed,
the public authority, in view of the true needs of the public
welfare, may point out more exactly what is licit and what
is not, for property-owners, in the use of their possessions ";
but: "Man's natural right to possess private property, and
to transmit it by inheritance, must remain intact and
inviolate, and cannot be taken away by the State: 'for man
precedes the State' (Leo XIII, *Rerum Novarum*, §6)."
"Wealth . . . must be so distributed among the various
individuals and classes of society, that the needs of all, of
which Leo XIII spoke, be thereby satisfied. . . . This
principle is violated by those of the wealthy who, practically
free from care in their own possessions, consider it quite
right to receive everything and the worker nothing; it is
violated also by those of the proletariat who demand for
themselves all the fruits of production, as being the work of
their hands." Though it is not unjust for contracts of
wages to be formed, they must be such as to support properly the workman and his family. The Pope inclines to
favour "corporations composed of the delegates of
workers and employers ": "Little reflection is required to
see [their] advantages: peaceful collaboration of various
classes, repression of Socialist organizations and efforts, the

moderating influence of the civil power." The Pope dwells on the modern advance of Socialism to Communism, and says: " To obtain their ends, Communists shrink from nothing and fear nothing; and when they have acquired power, it is monstrous and beyond belief how cruel and inhuman they show themselves to be." As to whether the Church " should somewhat moderate or attenuate Christian truth, so as to meet Socialism, as it were, half-way," the Pope says: " Such hope is vain. Those who wish to be apostles among the Socialists must preach the Christian truth whole and entire, openly and sincerely; without any connivance at error." " Religious Socialism, Christian Socialism, are expressions implying a contradiction in terms. No one can be at the same time a sincere Catholic and a Socialist properly so-called." Social reconstruction must be on the lines of the Catholic religion. " In order to bring back to Christ these whole classes of men who have denied Him, we must gather and train from amongst their very ranks auxiliary soldiers of the Church: men who well know their mentality and aspirations, and who, by kindly and fraternal charity, will be able to win their hearts. . . . It is especially for you, Venerable Brethren [the bishops], and that of your clergy, to seek diligently, to select prudently, and to train suitably, these lay apostles, amongst workmen and amongst employers."

PIUS XI, Encyclical *Caritate Christi Compulsi* (" On the Present Distress of the Human Race "; May 3, 1932). " If," said the Pope, " we pass in review the long and sorrowful sequence of woes that, as a sad heritage of sin, mark the stages of fallen man's earthly pilgrimage, from the Flood on, it would be hard to find spiritual and material distress so deep, so universal, as that which we are now experiencing. Even the greatest scourges that left indelible traces in the lives and memories of peoples, struck only one nation at a time. Now, on the contrary, the whole of humanity is held bound by the financial and economic crisis, so fast, that the more it struggles the harder seems the task of loosening its bonds." " The right order of Christian charity," he continues, " does not disapprove of lawful love of country, and a sentiment of justifiable nationalism; on the contrary, it controls, sanctifies, and enlivens them. If, however, egoism, abusing this love of country and exaggerating this sentiment of nationalism, insinuates itself into the relations between people and people, there is no excess that will not seem justified." " There were," he went on, " never lacking impious men, nor men who denied God; but they were relatively few, isolated, and individual. . . . To-day, however, atheism has spread already through large masses of the people." " We know very well, Venerable Brethren, that vain are all these efforts, and that, in the hour He has established, God will arise and His enemies shall be scattered (Psalm lxvii, 2). . . . But, none the less, confronted with so much impiety, such destruction of all the holiest traditions, such slaughter of immortal souls, such offences against the Divine Majesty, We cannot, Venerable Brethren, refrain from pouring out the bitter grief of Our soul." " In the name of the Lord, therefore, We beseech individuals and nations, in the face of such problems and in the throes of a conflict of such vital interest to mankind, to put aside that narrow individualism and base egoism that blinds even the most clear-sighted. . . . Let them all unite together, even at the cost of heavy sacrifices, to save themselves and mankind." " If those who, through the excessive production of manufactured goods, have fallen into unemployment and poverty, made up their minds to give the proper time to prayer, there is no doubt that work and production would be brought soon within reasonable limits, and that the conflict which now divides humanity into two great camps, struggling for transient interests, would be changed into a noble and peaceful contest for goods heavenly and eternal." The Pope therefore calls for prayer and penitence: " This year, let the Feast of the Sacred Heart of Jesus be for the whole Church one of holy rivalry of reparation and supplication. . . . The Divine Heart of Jesus cannot but be moved at the prayers and sacrifices of His Church, and He will finally say to His Spouse [the Church], weeping at His feet under the weight of so many griefs and woes: ' Great is thy faith; be it done to thee as thou wilt ' (Matt. xv, 28)."

PIUS XI, Encyclical *Acerba Animi* (" On the Wrongs to the Church in Mexico "; September 29, 1932). A conflict had broken out between the " left " parties and Catholics in Mexico. " The concern and sorrow which We feel," began the Pope, " at the present sad plight of human society at large in no way lessen Our special solicitude for Our beloved sons of the Mexican nation and for you, Venerable Brethren [" the Archbishops and Bishops and other local ordinances of the Federal States of Mexico," to whom this document was addressed], who are the more deserving of Our paternal regard because you have been so long harassed by grievous persecutions." " Whereas," he continued, " other Governments in recent times have been eager to renew agreements with the Holy See, that of Mexico frustrated every attempt to arrive at an understanding." " As a fresh affront to the Hierarchy of its Church, it was required that every State of the Confederation should determine the number of priests empowered to exercise the sacred ministry, in public or in private. In view of these intolerable and unjust injunctions, which would have subjected the Church in Mexico to the despotism of the State and of a Government hostile to the Church, you determined, Venerable Brethren, to suspend public worship [i.e., enforce an " Interdict "], and at the same time called on the faithful to make efficacious protest against the inequitable actions of the Government. For your apostolic firmness you were nearly all exiled from the Republic, and from the land of your banishment you had to witness the struggles and martyrdom of your priests and of your flock; whilst those very few amongst you who, almost by miracle, were able to remain in hiding in their own dioceses, succeeded in effectively encouraging the faithful with the splendid example of their own undaunted spirit." " In face of the firm and generous resistance of the oppressed, the Government began to give indications in various ways that it would not be averse to coming to an agreement. . . . We thought it best to profit by the occasion. . . . Unfortunately, as all know, Our wishes and desires were not followed by the peace and favourable settlement for which We had hoped. On the contrary, Bishops, priests, and faithful Catholics continued to be penalized and imprisoned, contrary to the spirit in which the *modus vivendi* had been established." " To approve such iniquitous laws, or spontaneously to give to them true and proper co-operation, is undoubtedly illicit and sacrilegious." " Let all, then, continue in that unity of purpose and obedience that We have praised." " To Our beloved Mexican sons We recommend with all Our heart the closest union with the Church and the Hierarchy [bishops]."

" POPE'S TERRIBLE SILENCE." In its issue for December 31, 1933, the London Sunday paper, *The People*, had, under this heading, the following paragraph: " Rome, Saturday.— The *Osservatore*, the Vatican organ, published a note stating that the year finished without any word from the Pope. ' This terrible silence,' it says, ' is a rebuke to the governments, whose jealousies, material interests, and passions, are poisoning the world so as to render futile and vain civil administration. In the piteous and criminal conditions in which the world finds itself the terrible silence of the Pope is the only appropriate gesture."

THE POPE AND THE CINEMAS. On June 29, 1936, Pope PIUS XI addressed to " Our Venerable Brethren, the Archbishops and Bishops of the United States of America, and to the other Ordinaries enjoying Peace and Communion with the Apostolic See," an Encyclical (*Vigilanti Curâ*) " On the Motion-Pictures." " In following with vigilant care," he said, " as Our pastoral office requires, the beneficent work of Our Brethren in the episcopate, and of the faithful, it has been highly pleasing to Us to learn of the fruits already gathered, and of the progress which continues to be made, by that prudent initiative launched more than two years ago as a holy crusade against the abuses of the motion-pictures, and entrusted in a special manner to the ' Legion of Decency.' " " The essential purpose of art," he continued, " its reason of existence, is to assist in the perfection of the moral personality, which is man; and for that reason it must be itself moral. And We concluded amidst the manifest approval of that elect body [a delegation of the International Federation of the Motion-Picture Press, received by the Pope in August, 1934]—the memory is still dear to Us—by recommending to them the necessity of making the motion-picture ' moral, an influence for good morals, an educator.' " Unfortunately: " It is a certainty, which can be verified readily, that the more marvellous the progress of the motion-picture art and industry, the more pernicious and deadly has it shown itself to morality and to religion and even to the very decencies of human society. The directors of the industry in the United States recognized this fact themselves when they confessed that the responsibility before the people and the world was their very own. In an agreement entered into by common accord in March,

1930, and solemnly sealed, signed and published in the Press, they formally pledged themselves to safeguard for the future the moral welfare of the patrons of the cinema. . . . Nevertheless, in spite of this wise and spontaneously taken decision, those responsible showed themselves incapable of carrying it into effect, and it appeared that the producers and the operators were not disposed to stand by the principles to which they had bound themselves. . . . In this crisis you, Venerable Brethren, were amongst the first to study the means of safeguarding the souls entrusted to your care, and you launched the ' Legion of Decency ' as a crusade for public morality designed to revitalize the ideals of natural and Christian rectitude. . . . Your leadership called forth the prompt and devoted loyalty of your faithful people, and millions of American Catholics signed the pledge of the ' Legion of Decency,' binding themselves not to attend any motion-picture which was offensive to Catholic moral principles or proper standards of living. . . . It is an exceedingly great comfort to Us to note the outstanding success of the crusade. Because of your vigilance, and because of the pressure which has been brought to bear by public opinion, the motion-picture has shown an improvement from the moral standpoint; crime and vice are portrayed less frequently; sin is no longer so openly approved and acclaimed; false ideals of life are no longer presented in so flagrant a manner to the impressionable minds of youth." Yet: " The problem of the production of moral films would be solved radically if it were possible for us to have production wholly inspired by the principles of Christian morality. . . . But since We know how hard it is to organize such an industry, especially because of considerations of a financial nature, and since, on the other hand, it is necessary to influence the production of all films so that they may contain nothing harmful from a religious, moral, or social viewpoint, therefore pastors of souls must exercise their vigilance over films wherever they may be produced and offered to Christian peoples." The pledge of the Legion of Decency must be repeated annually, and: " It will be necessary in each country for the bishops to set up a permanent national reviewing-office in order to be able to promote good motion-pictures, classify the others, and bring this judgment to the knowledge of priests and the faithful." "A mutual exchange of advice and information between the offices of the various countries will conduce to greater efficiency." "If the bishops of the world assume their share in the exercise of this painstaking vigilance over the motion-picture—and of this We, who know their pastoral zeal, have no doubt—they will accomplish for a certainty a great work for the protection of the morality of their people in their hours of leisure and recreation."

NAZI GERMANY. We have seen that the London *Catholic Herald* expressed the opinion that the experience of Pope Pius XI—when, before he became Pontiff, he was Papal Nuncio in Poland, and saw the Russian Bolshevist armies at the gates of Warsaw—gave him a permanent horror of Communism, and influenced his attitude to the rise of Hitler's Nazism in Germany. " Anything better than Atheistic Communism! " The Papacy, during its history, had had cause enough to look askance at German military despots. Its conflicts with the mediaeval Hohenstauffen (though the Papacy had won) had been grievous. The Protestant Reformation began in Germany, and was maintained by autocratic German rulers. Even in the nineteenth century, the *Kulturkampf* of Bismarck (though here again the Papacy had perhaps rather the better of it) had been a sore trial to Catholicism. The Pope, therefore, would hardly tend to support a regime like Hitler's. In any case, no regime of a " State totalitarian " type would meet with Papal approval except as a choice of evils. Such a system—even if it did not violate Papal teaching on social ideology in general—would subject the Church to the State: a condition of affairs abhorrent to the Papacy. Yet—" Anything better than Atheistic Communism! " If Hitler served to stave off that threat from Russia, he might be the less of two evils. So, when the Nazis attained power, German Catholics submitted. The historic Catholic *Centrum* party voluntarily dissolved itself. The Pope tried to come to an agreement with the Nazis on religious affairs in Germany; but his eventual disappointment at the result expressed itself in a vehement Encyclical (smuggled secretly into the Fatherland):—

PIUS XI, Encyclical *Mit Brennender Sorge* [it was in German, not, as usual, in Latin]: (" On the Condition of the Church in Germany "; March 14 [Passion Sunday], 1937). " With deep anxiety and increasing dismay," begins the Pope, " We have for some time past beheld the sufferings of the Church, and the steadily growing oppression of those men and women who, loyally professing their faith in thought and deed, have remained true to her amidst the people of that land to which St. Boniface once brought the light and glad tidings of Christ and the Kingdom of God." " In the summer of 1933, Venerable Brethren," he continued, " We accepted the offer made by the [Nazi] Government of the Reich to institute negotiations for a Concordat [Treaty] in connection with a proposal of the previous year; and, to the satisfaction of you all, We brought them to a conclusion with a solemn agreement. In this We were guided by the solicitude incumbent on Us to safeguard the freedom of the Church in the exercise of her apostolic mission in Germany and the salvation of the souls entrusted to her, and at the same time by the sincere wish of rendering an essential service to the progress and prosperity of the

German people. In spite of many serious misgivings at the time, We forced Ourselves to decide that We should not withhold our consent. . . . We do not refuse the hand of peace of Mother Church to anyone who does not himself reject it. If the tree of peace which We planted, with pure intention, in German soil has not borne the fruit We desired in the interests of your people, no one in the wide world who has eyes to see and ears to hear can say to-day that the fault lies with the Church and her Head. The lessons of the past years make it clear where the responsibility lies. They disclose machinations that from the beginning had no other aim than a war of extermination." " With amazement and deep aversion [it has become apparent that] to change the meaning of the agreement, to evade the agreement, to empty the agreement of all its significance, and finally more or less openly to violate the agreement, have been the unwritten laws of conduct of the other party." Yet: " Even to-day— when the open campaign waged against the denominational school guaranteed by the Concordat, when the nullification of the freedom of the vote for Catholics (who should have the right to decide in the matter of education), show the dreadful seriousness of the situation in a most important field of the Church's life and the unparalleled torment of consciences of believing Christians, Our pastoral care for the salvation of souls counsels Us not to leave unheeded even the slight prospects of return to a loyal adherence to a responsible agreement." " We thank you, Venerable Brethren, your priests and all the faithful, who have done and continue to do their duty in defending the sovereign rights of God against the aggressive neo-paganism that unfortunately in many cases is favoured in influential quarters." " In your districts, Venerable Brethren, voices are raised in ever louder chorus urging men on to leave the Church. . . . Leaving the Church, and the disloyalty to

Christ the King which it entails, is a particularly convincing and meritorious form of professing loyalty to the present [Nazi] State." "The repudiation," declares the Pope, "of the supernatural elevation of grace, on account of the supposedly peculiar German type of being, is an error, and an open challenge to a fundamental truth of Christianity." "Conscientious parents, aware of their duty in the matter of education, have a primary and original right to determine the education of the children given to them by God, in the spirit of the true Faith and in agreement with its spirit and ordinances. Laws, or other regulations concerning schools, that disregard the rights of parents guaranteed to them by the natural law; or by threat of violence nullify those rights, contradict the natural law and are utterly and essentially immoral." "We know that a free and secret ballot would in your case be equivalent to an overwhelming vote for the religious school." "He who *searches the heart and reins* (Psalm vii, 9) is Our witness that We have no more heart-felt wish than a restoration of a true peace between Church and State in Germany; but if, through a fault not Ours, there shall not be peace, the Church of God will defend her rights and her freedom, in the name of the Almighty whose arm even to-day is not shortened." Less than two months after the issue of this Encyclical the following news was published in the Press (we quote the London *Evening Standard*, May 1, 1937, which reproduced a despatch of the "Exchange" Agency):—"*Berlin*.—Herr Hitler, addressing 180,000 children at a May Day rally in Berlin to-day, made an important pronouncement on the demand of the Catholic Church for the education of Catholic youth. He said: 'There is only one German people and there can be only one German youth. There can be only one education and training of youth, and all those who cherish the hope that they will succeed in splitting up the youth will be disappointed. The German Reich will give up its youth to nobody, but will itself look after them and educate them. We want to educate youth to be able to withstand severity, suffering, and hardships.' "

SOVIET RUSSIA. Five days after the publication of the foregoing Encyclical complaining so bitterly of the German Nazi Government's failure to observe its Concordat with the Vatican, the Pope published another Letter, vehemently denouncing the whole system of the Communist regime in Russia:—

PIUS XI, Encyclical *Divini Redemptoris* (" On Atheistic Communism"; May 19, 1937). " The modern revolution," he began, " has actually broken out, or threatens almost everywhere, and it exceeds in amplitude and violence anything yet experienced in the preceding persecutions launched against the Church. Entire peoples find themselves in danger of falling back into a barbarism worse than that which oppressed the greater part of the world at the coming of the Redeemer. This all too imminent danger, Venerable Brethren, as you have already surmised, is Bolshevistic and Atheistic Communism, which aims at upsetting the social order and at undermining the very basis of Christian civilization. In the face of such a threat the Catholic Church could not and does not remain silent. . . . With reference to Communism, Our venerable predecessor, Pius IX, of holy memory, as early as 1846 pronounced a solemn condemnation. . . . Later on, another of Our predecessors, Leo XIII, in his Encyclical *Quod Apostolici Muneris*, defined Communism as ' the fatal plague which insinuates itself into the very marrow of human society only to bring about its ruin.' . . . During Our pontificate We too have frequently and with urgent insistence denounced the current trend to Atheism which is alarmingly on the increase. In 1924, when Our relief mission returned from the Soviet Union, We condemned Communism in a special Allocution [speech] which We addressed to the whole world. . . . Even to this hour the Papacy has continued faithfully to protect the sanctuary of the Christian religion, and it has called public attention to the perils of Communism more frequently and more effectively than any other public authority on earth." " Yet, despite Our frequent and paternal warnings, the peril only grows greater from day to day because of the pressure exerted by clever agitators. Therefore We believe it to be Our duty to raise Our voice once more, in a still more solemn missive. . . . We wish to expose once more, in a brief synthesis, the principles of Atheistic Communism as they are manifested chiefly in Bolshevism." The Pope then proceeds to a detailed survey. " The Communism of to-day," he says, " more emphatically than similar movements in the past, poses as the saviour of the poor. A pseudo-ideal of justice, of equality, and of fraternity in labour, impregnates all its doctrine." It is " based on the principles of dialectical and historical materialism advocated by Marx. . . . According to this doctrine, there is in the world only one reality—matter, the blind forces of which evolve into plant, animal, and man. . . . There is no room for the idea of God. . . . The Communists claim that the conflict which carries the world towards its final synthesis can be accelerated by man. Thus the class-struggle, with its consequent violent hate and destruction, takes on the aspect of a crusade for the progress of humanity. . . . Since, according to Communism, human personality is, so to say, a mere wheel in the machine of the universe, the natural rights which spring from it are denied to individuals and attributed to the community. . . . All forms of private property must be eradicated. . . . [Communism] makes of marriage and the family a purely artificial and civil institution. . . . Naturally, therefore, the notion of an indissoluble marriage-tie is repudiated. . . . The right of education is denied to parents, for it is conceived as the exclusive property of the community. . . . When all men have acquired finally the mentality necessary for this Utopia of a classless society, the political State . . . will have lost [according to Communists] all reason for its existence and will ' wither away '. . . . Such, Venerable Brethren, is the new gospel which Bolshevistic and Atheistic Communism offers the world as the glad tidings of deliverance and salvation! It is a system full of errors and illusions." For it, declares the Pope, " the way had been prepared already by the religious and moral destitution in which wage-earners had been left by ' liberal ' economics." He dilates on " the sorry effects of this propaganda " in Russia, Mexico, and Spain. " We are witnessing a struggle, coldblooded in purpose and mapped out to the last detail, between man and ' all that is called God ' (2 Thess., ii, 4)." " In making these observations it is no part of Our intention to condemn the peoples of the Soviet Union as a whole. For them We cherish the warmest paternal affection. . . . We blame only the system." With the system which he had thus described the Pope contrasts the doctrines of the Church:—" Contrast with it the true notion, already familiar to you, of the *civitas humana*, or human society, as taught by reason and revelation through the mouth of the Church, the Teacher of the nations. . . . Man has a spiritual and immortal soul. He is a person, marvellously endowed by his Creator with gifts of body and mind. . . . God alone is his last end, in this life and the next. . . . He has been endowed by God with many and varied prerogatives: the right to life, to bodily integrity, to obtain the necessary means of existence; the right to tend towards his ultimate goal [eternal life] in the path marked out for him by God; the right of association and the right to possess and use property. Just as matrimony and the right to its natural use are of divine origin, so likewise are the constitution and fundamental prerogatives of the family fixed and determined by the Creator. . . . Society is for man: not man for society. . . . Only man [the individual], and not society, in any form is endowed with reason and free will subject to the moral law." As to the economic system, the Pope refers back to Leo XIII's Encyclical *Rerum Novarum* and his own *Quadragesimo*. (See earlier in this book.) " A sound prosperity can be restored according to the true principles of a sane corporative order which respects the various grades of social authority, and in which all the vocational groups, fused into a harmonious whole, are inspired by the principle of the common good. . . . Catholic doctrine vindicates to the State the dignity and authority of a vigilant and provident defender of those divine and human rights on which the Sacred Scriptures and the Fathers of the Church insist so often. It is not true that all have equal rights in civil society. It is not true that there exists no lawful social hierarchy. . . . The enslavement of man, despoiled of his rights, the denial of the transcendental origin of the State and its authority, the horrible abuse of public power in the service of a collectivist terrorism are the very contrary of all that corresponds with natural ethics and the will of the Creator." The Church "maintains a constant equilibrium of truth and justice, . . . bringing into harmony the rights and duties of all parties." " There would be to-day neither Socialism nor Communism if the rulers of the nations had not scorned the teachings and maternal warnings of the Church. On the bases of Liberalism and Laicism they wished to build other social edifices which, powerful and imposing as they seemed at first, all too soon revealed the weakness of their founda-

E

tions." "The most urgent need of the present day is the energetic and timely application of remedies which effectively will ward off the catastrophe that daily grows more menacing. . . . The fundamental remedy to-day lies in a sincere renewal of private and public life according to the principles of the Gospel." "Even in Catholic countries there are still too many who are Catholics only in name." "All Christians, rich or poor, must keep their eyes fixed on heaven, remembering that ' we have not here a lasting city, but we seek one that is to come ' (Hebrews, xiii, 14)." Wealth should be more equitably distributed, so that there shall not be " thousands of the needy, victims of real misery for various reasons beyond their control, and so many around them who spend huge sums of money on useless things and frivolous amusement." "A ' charity ' which deprives the working-man of the wages due to him, is not charity at all, but only its empty name and hollow semblance. The wage-earner is not to receive in alms what is due in justice. . . . So We turn in a special way to you, Christian employers and industrialists, whose problem is often so hard because you are burdened with the heavy heritage of an unjust economic regime. . . . It is unfortunately true that the manner of acting in certain Catholic circles has done much to shake the faith of the working classes in the religion of Jesus Christ." "It is of the very essence of social justice to demand from each individual all that is needful for the common good. . . . Therefore each person must be supplied with all that is necessary for the exercise of his social functions. . . . But social justice cannot be said to have been satisfied so long as working-men are denied a wage that will enable them to secure proper sustenance for themselves and their families." There must be greater propaganda of Catholic social principles, it being remembered that " Communism is intrinsically wrong, and no one who would save Christian civilization may give it assistance in any understanding whatsoever." "To apply the remedies thus briefly indicated, Jesus Christ, our Divine King, has chosen priests as the first-line ministers and messengers of His Gospel. . . . [Priests] must go to the working-man." Next: "We extend our paternal invitation to Our beloved sons among the laity who are doing battle in the ranks of Catholic Action. . . . They will be the first and immediate apostles of their fellow workers." With them will be "auxiliary forces." "All diligence should be exercised by States to prevent within their territories the ravages of an anti-God campaign which shakes society to its very foundations—for there can be no authority on earth unless the authority of the Divine Majesty is recognised." "At the same time the State must allow the Church full liberty to fulfil her divine and spiritual mission."

THE UNITED STATES OF AMERICA. On the death of Pope Pius XI Cardinal Pacelli was elected as his successor, and took the name, Pius XII. He is the reigning Pontiff at the time of the writing of this book. On November 1, 1939 ("the first year of Our pontificate"), he addressed a jubilant yet monitory Encyclical to the Catholics of the United States of America, who were celebrating the 150th anniversary of the establishment of the hierarchy of Catholic bishops in that country. The Encyclical was addressed "to Our beloved sons, William O'Connell, Cardinal-Archbishop of Boston; Denis Dougherty, Cardinal-Archbishop of Philadelphia; and to Our Venerable Brethren, the Archbishops, Bishops, and Other Local Ordinaries of the United States of America in Peace and Communion with the Apostolic See:—

PIUS XII, Encyclical *Sertum Laetitiae* ("On the 150th Anniversary of the U.S.A. Hierarchy"; November 1,

1939). " Over wide-tracked oceans Our thoughts go,"
began the Pope, " to participate in the sacred rejoicing in
which you are engaged.   We stand in spirit near you as you
celebrate a century and a half of good omen which have
passed since your Hierarchy began."   " When John Car-
roll, an American citizen, was made Bishop of Baltimore—
thus being the first of your episcopal prelates—the ranks of
Catholicism in your country were few and poor.   Moreover, the position of the United States themselves was so
perilous that it appeared dubious whether they could continue as a single Community.   There had been a bitter war;
the exchequer was burdened with grave debt, industry was
stagnant; the people, divided with faction, were wearied by
troubles.   To save his country was the task of a man of
courage and clear thought, the celebrated George Washington—who was an intimate friend of the new Bishop of
Baltimore. . . . The Bishop had the noble help of priests
who had been driven to America from Europe by persecution.   They rallied to his help and sowed the seeds of what
was to become a noble harvest."   " When [in 1889] a
century had elapsed, Our memorable predecessor, Leo XIII,
addressed to you his Encyclical *Longinqua Oceani*, reviewing
the Church's progress in your country, and giving warnings
and advice. . . . [Since then], the life nourished in you
by the Holy Spirit is strong and healthy."   The Pope proceeded to enumerate the many American Catholic Societies
and activities.   " It would be a long story to number the
roll of all those societies of the laity which have won
fadeless glory here.   Catholic Action; the Congregations
of Our Lady; the Confraternity of Christian Doctrine:
all are rich in good works—richer still in future prospects.
So also is the Holy Name Society. . . . All these many
branches of Catholic activity in one and another way, as
the moment calls, are controlled by a central council:

the National Catholic Welfare Conference." "Religious [monks, Jesuits, etc.] of every Order—adorned with all virtues, vie in labour in God's harvest. Religious women, also (lilies in the divine garden), are enflamed with holy love and nobly labour for the Gospel." Yet, warns the Pope, there are dangers: "All over the world there is—a root of troubles—an ignoring of God; neglect of His law. . . . Blind excess of egoism; thirst for pleasure; drunkenness; extravagant fashions in dress; frequency of crime, even amongst youth; lust for power; disregard of the poor; desire for ill-gotten wealth," etc. It is needful to emphasize the love of marriage and the family; to discountenance divorce and discourage "mixed marriages" (i.e., of Catholics with non-Catholics). There must be charity of rich to poor. The teachings of Leo XIII's Encyclical *Rerum Novarum* must be followed. The Pope ends: "With the sure prayer that you and your flocks will daily make great progress in all good things, and will have a rich reward in your celebrations, We impart Our Apostolic Blessing."

AN AMERICAN PROBLEM. Our survey of Papal teachings will have brought out the fact that there is—to express it moderately—some discrepancy between them and modern "secularist democracy." That fact cannot but show itself in a country so democratic as is the U.S.A. Naturally, therefore, American Catholics must be exercised to reconcile the Church's teachings, on sociology, with the institutions of their country. An interesting article on that subject may here be examined. The *Catholic Digest* is one of those many "symposium-magazines" that have become so popular: publications made up of articles, or summaries of articles, from other publications. It is issued from Minnesota, U.S.A., but has editions for Dublin and Belgium. It seems to be popular also in Great Britain amongst

Catholics.   In the January, 1947, number was an article by John Courtney Murray, S.J., entitled " Separation of Church and State."   It was " condensed from *America* "— a popular U.S.A. Catholic Magazine—and was an effort to show that American Catholics not only may acquiesce in, for the sake of expediency, but also may support, *as good in itself*, the U.S.A. principle of full religious freedom and no legal establishment of any religious body.

The first clause of the First Amendment of the U.S.A. Constitution declares that " Congress shall make no law respecting the establishment of religion or prohibiting the free exercise thereof."   This Amendment was enacted shortly after the setting-up of the independence of the States, and it caused the disestablishment of the Anglican and Congregationalist bodies, which previously had enjoyed legal privileges in some districts.   The task of Father Murray's article was that of reconciling the teaching of Catholicism, on social questions, with the forequoted clause. He said: " The confused polemist can, of course, make use of the formula with great effect: ' Catholics support separation of Church and State in the U.S.; they oppose it in Spain.   You see, therefore, what unprincipled power-politicians they are; they act solely on immoral grounds of expediency.'   The argument has gone over in a big way of late in the U.S.; the confused polemists have popularized this confusion with great success.   But the whole success has been due to the ambiguity of the slogan, ' Separation of Church and State.' "

According to Father Murray, that " slogan " (or " formula ") has two possible meanings.   On the European continent it signifies " a ' lay ' State, predicated on atheistic, or agnostic principles, militantly aggressive in opposition to religion."   It is only that form of separation that Catholics oppose.   The form of separation in the U.S.A. is very different.   It is " of a peculiarly American form, in consequence of a natively American and entirely valid theory of religious liberty.   That is why Catholics support it, not only in practice (as expedient for themselves) but in principle (as sound in itself)."   That " natively American theory, entirely valid," is that " the U.S.A., by virtue of the First Amendment, is a ' lay ' State . . . in consequence of ethical principle, and in the light of the American situation, and for the sake of its own end.   It retains proper authority over the lay life of its citizens—their life as citizens; but it has no authority over their religious lives.   In Madison's phrase, it is ' not a competent judge of religious truths,' and it has no power to enforce acceptance of them.   As a layman in matters of religion, the American State respects the religious authority inherent in the consciences of its citizens.   The [religious] authorities conflict; but the State stands outside their conflicts.   It cannot silence any particular religious utterance, because it is the utterance of one of its citizens; on the other hand, it cannot espouse any religious utterance, because it is the utterance of *only one* of its citizens."   Such, then, is the conception of Church and State which Father Murray maintains that a U.S.A. Catholic may " support . . . as sound in itself."   The reader of Father Murray will ask, however, how does that theory compare with the historic practice of Catholicism, and with present-day (not merely mediaeval) Papal teaching?   From the very first days of its rise to power, the Catholic Church, headed by the Popes, declared it to be a duty of the State to uphold the one, true, Catholic Faith.   The State was required to suppress heresy.   In modern times (as we have seen) the Papal utterances on Church and State have reiterated that principle.   How can it be reconciled with the " American " conception which Father Murray says is " sound in itself "?   At the end of his ingenious article

Father Murray's essential fallacy discloses itself. He says: "They [Catholics] have, it is true, their own theology of religious liberty; so do [? have] Protestants. But neither Catholic nor Protestant theology is written into the First Amendment." True!—but, if the American Constitution were framed on Catholic principles, Catholic "theology of religious liberty" *would be* "written into" *that Constitution*—in which case the First Amendment would cease to exist. In short, American Catholics cannot logically support the "U.S.A. conception" as "sound in itself," but only as "expedient"—as Leo XIII expressed it, "until happier times." A view different from that of Father Murray may be quoted: "Constitutions can be changed, and non-Catholic sects may decline to such a point that the political proscription of them may become feasible and expedient. What protection would they then have against a Catholic State? The latter could logically tolerate only such religious activities as were confined to the members of the dissenting group. It could not permit them to carry on general propaganda nor accord their organization certain privileges that had formerly been extended to all religious corporations, for example, exemption from taxation."— From *The State and the Church*; written and edited for the Department of Social Action of the National Catholic Welfare Council by John A. Ryan, D.D., LL.D., Professor of Moral Theology at the Catholic University of America, and Moorehouse F. X. Millar, S.J., and carrying the Imprimatur ("It may be printed") of the diocesan censor, New York, 1922; page 38.

Clearly, Catholic social teaching conflicts in principle, in some vital matters, with the ideology of the United States. That, however, is only part of a general problem evident all over the world. The Church would say that, as the Ambassador of Christ and the Teacher of Eternal Verity, it has been always in more or less conflict with the spirit of its times, and that that fact is simply because it is divinely-originated and the world is sinful. On the other hand, secular thinkers would say that the Church is a narrow, sectional body opposed to progress and freedom. Whatever the truth of the matter, the fact of the existence of a conflict of ideals cannot be denied.

CATHOLIC ACTION. Returning over "the trackless ocean" to Great Britain, we must go back for a time into the Pontificate of Pope Pius XII's immediate predecessor, Pius XI. That Pope, as we have seen, was very ardent in advocating "Catholic Action." Acting on his directives, in May, 1934, the Catholic Archbishops and Bishops of England and Wales issued a Joint Pastoral Letter, which we may reproduce here (from the London *Catholic Herald*, May 26, 1934):—

"Our Sovereign Pontiff, Pope Pius XI, indicating the remedy for our present discontents in the troubled state of the post-war [war of 1914-1918] world, has spoken of the necessity of Catholic Action with a frequency, an insistency, and a solemnity, which must needs command our earnest attention.

"He himself has given us the authentic definition of Catholic Action as the participation and collaboration of the laity with the Apostolic Hierarchy [the Bishops] in matters affecting the rights and vital interests of Holy Mother Church. Notwithstanding this clear pronouncement, clouds of misconception have gathered round the term Catholic Action, which has been taken by some as connoting some form of ecclesiastical aggression, by others as a species of masked political activity. In reality the movement is essentially pacific, being of a spiritual character, aiming at bringing the lives of the members of all Catholic societies into closer conformity with the principles of our holy religion. Catholic Action is in fact radicated [rooted] in spirituality, deriving its motive power precisely from the personal sanctification of its adherents, imparting to them and to the Church as a whole that interior peace which the world can neither give nor take away. But this inward sanctification must manifest itself outwardly in the world, both for its own sake and for the sake of the world. For its own sake, since piety limited to the inner sphere of thought, and the interior life of the soul, without expressing itself and becoming audible and visible when opportunity offers, is apt to dwindle and become enfeebled. For the sake of the world, inasmuch as, being children of light, it is our duty to let that light shine before other men so that they too may walk in its life-giving rays. For Catholic Action, though rooted in spirituality, is not mere passivity, but activity: activity open, vigorous, and persistent to further God's kingdom on earth. Though not of the world in origin, its place is in the world to be seen by the world and be felt by the world.

" Assuredly interests of a purely material and temporal character are not its object. The Holy Father [the Pope] has stressed the fact time and again, in his public pronouncements, that Catholic Action is above and beyond all politics, whether national or international. He has laid it down explicitly that abstention from every form of political activity is a fundamental law of this world-wide movement. The guarantee of its spiritual character and aims is to be found in the Holy Father's statement that ' Catholic Action is, and always will be, dependent upon the episcopate.' For it is the wise ruling of the Church that those who desire to promote her welfare or defend her interests shall do so only under the sanction and guidance of legitimate ecclesiastical authority. Though directed by the clergy, the exercise of Catholic activity must in large measure devolve upon the laity. Here in England in the past clergy and laity have participated most successfully in many and various undertakings, and it is proposed now to consolidate and enlarge that participation. . . .

" We propose to establish a National Board of Catholic Action consisting of the members of the Hierarchy of England and Wales under the presidency of His Eminence the Cardinal-Archbishop of Westminster. . . .

" Under ecclesiastical control and guidance Catholic Action will be directed to watching the Press and broadcast utterances for misrepresentations with regard to the Catholic Faith and practice; it will sedulously safeguard the interests of Catholic schools in the face of threatened inimical legislation; it will defend the principles of Catholic morality against the insidious propaganda of the new paganism; it will strive to secure for Catholics adequate representation on public bodies; it will aim at co-ordinating and intensifying all the means hitherto employed to bring the knowledge of our Holy Faith to the minds of our fellow-countrymen both by the spoken and the written word. . . . If the numerous Catholic societies which exist in this country be linked in this way in corporate unity we shall have a powerful organization for moulding public opinion and for asserting and defending our Catholic rights. . . ."

Commenting on this Pastoral, the London Catholic weekly, the *Universe* (May 25, 1934, in an article headed " The Call to Action "), said: " In this week of Pentecost we may well remember that Catholic Action is, quite directly, the work of the Holy Spirit Himself. . . . The book of the Acts of the Apostles is truly the Gospel of the Holy Ghost . . . simply the record of the first corporate Catholic Action, in all its pristine vigour—the model for the activity of the Catholic people in all succeeding ages."

SPAIN. In considering the terrible civil war in Spain,
it is needful to see it in the light of history.   It must be
borne always in mind that *for nearly 800 years* Spain was
the scene of war between two rival races and religions:
Catholicism and Islam.   Not until 1492 was the last vestige
of Muslim rule driven from the peninsula.   As a result of
this centuries-long conflict, Spaniards inevitably tended
" to go to extremes."   This has been seen in all their
disputes.   In order to avoid suspicion of quoting anti-
Catholic opinion, we may use the statements of an able
booklet published (June, 1938) by the Catholic Truth
Society, London: *The Catholic Church in Spain from 1800
till To-day*, by A. A. Parker, M.A., Fellow of Gonville and
Caius College, Cambridge.   It is very temperately written
and gives a vivid survey of 131 years:—

" The Church," says Mr. Parker (p. 3), " has been forced
on to one side by the opposition of the other, which repre-
sents a political system that, in its different historical forms,
has consistently attacked her."   In the year 1700 " the ad-
vent of the Bourbon dynasty, in the person of Philip V, laid
Spain open to the active influence of French ideas " (p. 4).
This " paved the way to Liberalism " (p. 4).   There were
disputes with the Papacy.   Even the Spanish clergy itself
was affected: " Most of the prominent canonists [teachers of
Church law] and several of the bishops were openly anti-
Roman, toying with the idea of a national schismatic
Church " (p. 5).   There was " a decline of religion, due to
the invasion of deism, scepticism, and materialist philosophy.   But it is important to stress the fact that at this
time the great mass of the people remained untouched by
these new ideas, both by the irreligion of their rulers and
the ' Jansenism ' of a section of the clergy " (p. 5).   Then
came the invasion by Napoleon Bonaparte.   " The people
rose in arms [to resist it], their resistance being organized

largely by the bishops and clergy " (pp. 6–7). At some places, however, there were anti-religious outbreaks: " In 1809–1810 the Bishop of Coria was executed, the cathedral of Solsona was burned; at Urcles some nuns were mas- sacred " (p. 7). Cortes (a Parliament) at Cadiz drew up a Liberalistic Constitution. The Inquisition was abolished. " This first phase of Liberal government [, however,] was of short duration. In 1814, with the acclamation of the people, all this legislation, together with the Constitution, was annulled by Ferdinand VII on his return from cap- tivity " (p. 9). In 1820, however, came a military revolt, followed by anti-Church legislation and a diplomatic break with the Papacy: but—" This second period of Liberal rule collapsed in 1823, the Government offering no resis- tance to the French Army, sent by the Holy Alliance to restore Ferdinand to personal rule. The Liberal legislation was once more rescinded, except that the Inquisition was not this time restored " (p. 12). Ferdinand died in 1833, and " there began the definite period of revolution which was to last with brief intervals until 1844, and which was to prove permanent in its effects " (p. 12). In 1836 there was a great seizure of Church property by the State. Bishops were appointed without agreement with the Pope. When the Liberals, in 1844, lost power to the Moderados (Con- servatives), " the next nine years [were] a period of relative peace for the Church " (p. 16).

Mr. Parker recognizes (p. 16) that " it cannot be denied that the external organization of the Church at the begin- ning of the nineteenth century did need reform "—though he thinks the Liberals used wrong methods in attempting it. In 1851 a Concordat was concluded with Rome. It " affirmed that Catholicism was the official religion of Spain, and the public practice of any other was prohibited " (p. 24). " The Church found herself implicated in politics and her welfare identified with that of one [Conservative] party " (p. 27). In 1854 a revolution returned the Liberals to power, and relations with Rome were again broken. The Liberals fell in 1856, but there was another revolution in 1868. A Republic was proclaimed in 1873, but the monarchy (King Alfonso XII) returned in 1874. There was an agreement with Rome. From then until 1923 two parties (" Liberal " and " Conservative ") alternated in power by the " rotatative " (agreement) system. " Outwardly, therefore, the Church enjoyed a comparatively long period of peace, but this peace was as artificial as the political system which guaranteed it " (p. 31). The Church " was still in practice tied to a particular political form of the State, and identified with it by its opponents " (p. 31). In 1909 there was a " left " revolt in Barcelona. [In relation to it, a statement of the non-Catholic case may be seen in the contemporary book, *The Martyrdom of Ferrer*, by Joseph McCabe. It is a useful " check " on Mr. Parker's pamphlet—and Parker's on McCabe's!] " In April, 1931, the transformation of Spain into a Republic was peacefully effected. Before the first month was out, however, rioting occurred in Madrid, in which six churches, religious houses [convents], and colleges, were destroyed by fire " (p. 32). " The new Constitution, with its attendant legislation, completed the laicization of the State " (p. 32). In 1936 " chaos gave way to civil war " (p. 36).

It is clear that a basic cleavage of ideologies existed in Spain; as Mr. Parker says: " The vicious circle was evident in all respects: The anti-clericalism of the Liberals made the Church quite naturally anti-Liberal; the anti-Liberalism made the Liberals anti-religious." There was " a fundamental cleavage in the nation " (p. 40).

In a pamphlet issued in October, 1938, by the Catholic Truth Society, London (*The Conflict in Spain*, by the

Marquis de Merry del Val), a passionate defence was made of the Spanish Church, and it was stated (p. 8) that " the issue in Spain, therefore, is not being fought out between Democracy and Fascism. It is the despairing effort of a virile people to throw off the stranglehold of Moscow." " General Franco and his National Movement . . . represent the principles of Morality and Justice, the essential foundations of Civilization. It is in their name that they exercise not *reprisals* or acts of revenge, . . . but the right and duty of *punishment* and *vindication* of justice " (p. 12). Franco's cause " should be that of every right-thinking man and woman in this honest land [Great Britain] " (p. 15). Yet Don de Merry del Val candidly admitted (p. 5) that " A recent book by Father Peyré, S.J., shows exactly what percentage of practising Catholics was in Spain. The majority was content to bear the name without the duties." In short, there was a fatal cleavage of life.

The Catholic Church, then, supported General Franco. On September 14, 1936, Pope PIUS XI delivered a speech to a pilgrimage of Bishops, priests, nuns, and layfolk, refugees from Spain. He said:—" Your presence here, beloved sons exiled from that Spain, dear to you and to Ourself, that is in such tribulation, fills Our heart with a medley of feelings so opposed and contrasted that it is impossible to give them adequate expression at this moment. Now We would weep for the profound bitterness which afflicts Our heart; again We would rejoice for the sweet and proud joy which consoles Us and makes Us jubilant." " You have been robbed," he continued, " and despoiled of all things; you have been hunted and sought unto death." " What can we say to praise you, venerated Bishops and priests, persecuted and wronged just because you are ' ministers of Christ and dispensers of the mysteries of God ' (i. Cor., iv, (1?" " We must say to you, as the apostle said to your earliest predecessors in the glory of martyrdom: ' my joy and my crown ' (Phil., iv, 1)." " God knows that war, even in the last tragic circumstances, is always something so fearful and so inhuman. . . . What is to be said when we are confronted with fratricidal strife? " The Spanish conflict was provoked by " those forces [Communist] which already have given proof of their quality in the attempts to subvert established order of every kind, from Russia to China, from Mexico to South America." " Our Benediction, above any mere political or mundane consideration, goes out, in a special manner, to all those who have assumed the difficult and dangerous task of defending and restoring the rights and honour of God and of Religion." (This speech was published as a pamphlet by the Catholic Truth Society, London—October, 1936— *The Pope on the Spanish Terror*; Catalogue number, " H. 265.")

On July 1, 1937, " the Feast of the Precious Blood of Our Lord Jesus Christ," a Joint Letter " to the Bishops of the Whole World, Concerning the War in Spain," was issued, signed by Isidro, Cardinal Gomá y Tomas, Archbishop of Toledo, Primate of Spain; Cardinal Ilundain y Esteban, Archbishop of Seville; the Archbishops of Valencia, Burgos, Saragossa, Santiago, Granada, and Majorca; thirty-five Bishops; and five Vicars-Capitular (administrators of vacant Sees). It said: " In times of tribulation Catholic peoples are wont to lend each other mutual help. . . . The Spanish Episcopate, which has been so cruelly tried in its members, in its clergy, and in its churches, desires to-day, by means of this collective document, to express its gratitude for the great manifestation of charity which has come to it from all parts of the world. . . . It is a fact, as we know from abundant documentary evidence, that a large sector of foreign opinion has not the

least idea of what has in fact been occurring in our country.
. . . What distresses us most is that a considerable part
of the Catholic Press in other countries should have con-
tributed to this deviation from the truth." " The Spanish
war is the result of the struggle between irreconcilable
principles; in its very origins are involved the gravest
questions of historical, religious, juridical, and moral order."
" Ever since the year 1931, the Spanish Episcopate has set
the highest example of civic and apostolic prudence. In
conformity with the tradition of the Church, and following
the principles of the Holy See, it ranged itself resolutely on
the side of the constituted authorities, and endeavoured to
collaborate with them for the common good. And despite
the repeated commission of offences against persons,
property, and rights of the Church, it never swerved from
its purpose of non-interference with the long-established
regime of harmony with the State." Yet: " Such is human
nature, and such the order of Providence—for which no
substitute has yet been found—that war, though one of
the most terrible scourges of our race, is sometimes a heroic
remedy, and the only practicable method of restoring human
affairs according to the standards of justice and re-establishing the Kingdom of Peace. Therefore the Church, though
the daughter of the Prince of Peace, blesses the emblems of
war, has founded the military Orders, and has organized
Crusades against the enemies of the Faith. But this is not
the case here. The Church has neither desired this war
nor provoked it. . . . It is true that thousands of her
sons, obeying the dictates of their conscience and of their
patriotism, and on their own personal responsibility, rose
in armed revolt in order to safeguard the principles of human
justice and religion which for ages past inspires the nation's
life; but anyone who accuses the Church of having provoked this war, or of having conspired for it, or even of not

F

having done all in her power to prevent its outbreak, is either ignorant of, or falsifies, the reality." "This war has been brought about by the rashness, the mistakes, and perhaps the malice and the cowardice of those who could have prevented it had they governed the nation with justice. To set aside causes of lesser moment, it was the lawmakers of 1931, and, later, the executive power of the State with its governmental practices, that persisted in forcing the path of our history to deviate in a direction quite foreign to the nature and needs of the national spirit, and, in particular, to the religious sense predominant in the country. The Constitution, and the secularist laws which gave expression to the spirit of the Constitution, amounted to one continuous and violent attack upon the national conscience. . . . At the same time, on numerous and grave occasions, the authorities surrendered their power to the populace. The burning of the churches in Madrid and in the provinces in May, 1931; the revolts of October, 1934, especially in Catalonia and Asturias, where for a fortnight anarchy reigned supreme; the turbulent period between February and July, 1936, which witnessed the destruction or profanation of 411 churches and the commission of some 3,000 serious transgressions of a political and social character —all these presaged the total failure of authority, which again and again could be seen succumbing to the force of the secret powers that impeded its functions." "Another powerful nation—Russia—was combining with the Communists of Spain, and, by means of stage and screen, through the introduction of foreign rites and customs, by casting a spell over people's minds, and by material bribery, was preparing the popular mind for the outbreak of a Revolution the date of which could be predicted almost to the day. . . . Such are the facts. Let them be read side by side with the teaching of St. Thomas [Aquinas: the greatest theologian of Catholicism] concerning the legitimacy of defensive resistance by force, and let each judge with just judgment." "The national conscience felt the legal means of redress to be exhausted, so that no other method was left of maintaining order and peace but that of force. . . . On July 18th, 1936, came the [Franco] military revolt and the outbreak of the war that is still in progress. . . . This movement, and the Communist Revolution, are two facts which, if the nature of the war is to be fairly judged, cannot be separated. Taking place, as they did, at the same initial moment of the conflict, they have, from the very first, marked the profound division separating the two Spains now at grips upon the field of battle." [The war is] "a fierce conflict between a people cleft in twain. On the side of the [Franco] insurgents was a spiritual force rising in the defence of order, social peace, traditional civilization, and the Mother Country, and, most noticeably, as regards a large proportion of the people, in defence of religion. On the other side was a materialistic force—Marxist, Communist, or Anarchist—which desired to substitute for the old civilization of Spain, with all its distinguishing characteristics, the brand-new 'civilization' of the Russian Soviets." "The Church, despite her pacific spirit and the fact that she neither desired the war nor had any part in bringing it about, could not remain indifferent during the struggle. Her doctrine and her spirit, the instinct of self-preservation and the experience of Russia, made this impossible." "As regards the future, we cannot foretell what will happen at the conclusion of the struggle. . . . We should be the first to regret it if, for the irresponsible autocracy of a Parliament, were substituted the more terrible autocracy of a dictatorship without roots in the nation. We cherish the legitimate hope that this will not come to pass."

"A struggle between irreconcilable principles." "A fierce conflict between a people cleft in twain." "The profound division separating the two Spains." Such, in truth, was the secret of the Spanish civil war. It is, on a world-wide scale, the secret of perturbations, uneasiness, and menace, in many other lands.

THE SECOND WORLD WAR (1939-1945). The first Encyclical of Pope Pius XII was issued—he being newly-elected after the death of Pius XI—soon after the outbreak of the second world war:—

PIUS XII, Encyclical *Summi Pontificatus* (" On ' Darkness over the Earth ' "; October 20, 1939). "Our predecessor, of undying memory—Leo XIII—forty years ago," said the new Pontiff, ". . . recommended to all the world that it be consecrated to the Sacred Heart of Jesus. . . . Let us glance at how, since then, the events of the world and the developments of human thought, have presented themselves as viewed from the standpoint of eternity. How have they risen?—how declined?" "Humanity has become engulfed in merely earthly ambitions, and misery, exhaustion, have resulted." "We place this, Our first Encyclical, under the flag and standard of Christ the King." "We place on record Our deep pleasure at the way Emperors, Kings, and other chiefs of States, have, in the name of their subjects, given Us their noblest marks of respect. With especial joy we can now [because of the Lateran Treaty re-establishing a measure of Papal temporal rule] include Italy. . . . A glorious event has resulted—for the good of Italy and of the whole Christian world—in a new and happy state of affairs." "Yet, as We indite the words, comes the awful news that—despite Our prayers—the fiery storm of war has burst. . . . We are sick at heart when we think of the grim harvest being sown." "Existing troubles and miseries confirm strikingly the contentions of Christian thinkers; . . . for it is repudiation of Christian doctrine which has led to them." The Pope put the blame largely on the Reformation of the sixteenth century: "In past ages European peoples were conjoined by unity of Christian belief, which elevated, civilized, and raised them. A time arrived, however, when many of Christendom abandoned the teaching of the unerring Church. Afterwards they went even farther—giving up even belief in our Saviour as Divine. Thus came a general decline of religion. We read in the Gospel that, when our Lord was on the Cross, 'there was darkness over the face of the earth' (Matt., xxvii, 45). It was a sad parable of what always occurs when faith is lost." "Men failed to realize that, in giving up Divine Law and Christ's wise precepts, they would place themselves at the mercy of mere abject worldly wisdom." "True, there were conflicts, revolutions, and disastrous wars, even when Europe was united in one Christian tradition—but never such woes as in our own times." "Sight has been lost of that love and kinship which should unite humanity." "It is right that, as nations advance in culture, they should differ in ways of conducting their affairs; but never should the essential unity of mankind be forgotten. Each nation should contribute to general human well-being by its special part in the variety." "It is a very pernicious error to dissociate civil rule from that of God—upon whom it depends as its first author and highest authority. If every freedom is given to the fallen will of man, with no restraint but human speculation, and if the civil power is not required to observe God's Laws, things become even worse. The civil power will usurp the supreme rights belonging alone to the Creator." "There is, however, an inescapable law which will bring nemesis. It is, that no institution can evade ruin if it is out of proper proportion. . . . Such must be the case when the civil power either denies or disregards the Supreme Law-giver." "That man is an enemy of real progress who regards the State as the supreme end of all things—whether such unlimited power be given to the State by the laws of a nation, of some special class, or by the seizure of authority by a despot responsible to none. The State also errs when it takes to itself all private industry—for such industries call for many rules peculiar to each, and evils result from their removal from private control." Another error is that of regarding the education of children as chiefly "to produce in all ways a sort of 'civic consciousness,' for the political future of the country. . . . There is a decay of the precious treasures of family life." "Secular education" is "the training of the young by neglecting or repudiating the Christian religion, and is a treachery against 'the King of kings, and Lord of lords' (i Tim., vi, 15; Apocalypse, xix, 16). It will produce a woeful harvest." "The theory which would make the State the possessor of limitless powers, will bring fatal results. . . . It severs the ties of commonwealths, emasculates the laws of nations, and wars against peace and good will. . . . Absolute, irresponsible power for rulers is the foe of our human nature." "This war," continued the Pope, "at its conclusion, will see new pacts, new plans of relations amongst nations. Will they be in the spirit of fair equity all round, reconstituting peace, or will they repeat former failures? . . . Victors' hearts—hardened—may have no place for calmness, for 'long views.' . . . The cry may be, 'Woe to the defeated!' This will produce only injustice." "It is the Catholic Church's duty to renovate the minds of peoples in the new conditions and needs of this age." One method will be by "Catholic Action, organized in various ways to aid the task of the

Church. . . . It will supplement and complete the work of the clergy, by following the guidance of the Pope and local Bishops." "We, as Christ's Vicar on earth—the vicegerent of the One who was 'the Prince of Peace' (Isaiah, ix, 6)—call on rulers of States to give to the Church that full freedom to which she is entitled. Let her conduct her work of education; instil truth into men's minds and justice into their heads." The Pope explained how he had striven to prevent war: "We left no stone unturned, no avenue unexplored to prevent, by any means at Our disposal in Our Apostolic office, a resort to arms. The door must not be closed on any chance of settling matters in dispute in a way honourable to all concerned. . . . But our advice was listened to apparently with respect—and was not taken."

PIUS XII, Allocution (Speech), *In Questo Giorno* (" On Conditions of Peace "; December 24, 1939). Addressing the Sacred College of Cardinals on Christmas Eve of the first year of "World War Two," Pope Pius XII, after dwelling on the holy significance of the season, went on: " The disaster of war, terrible beyond speech—which Pius XI foresaw with sorrow and nobly sought to avert— is now on us, filling Our heart with profound affliction." He said that the coming of war was a result of failure to honour agreements: " The questions pending amongst nations were far from beyond solution, but there was absence of confidence in the efficacy of promises made, and of agreements reached." How, then, can a just peace eventually be made? The Pope laid down five " peace points," prefacing them by saying that " there must be no inflexible refusal to negotiate peace on a favourable opportunity, when necessary guarantees and safeguards are present." His " five points " were: (1) There must be for all nations, great or small, the right to life and independence; (2) There must be mutually agreed and progressive disarmament; (3) To prevent violations of agreements, and other former errors, there must be set up some judicial institution to guarantee fulfilment of engagements, and, when necessary, to revise and amend them; (4) There must be protection of minorities, even, when called for, by revision of treaties; (5) But " even the best regulations will fail unless there is submission to the law of God and the Christian ideal of universal love." On Easter Sunday, 1941, the Pope broadcast over the Vatican Radio a special message, as thus reported in the London *News Chronicle*, Monday, April 14:—

" POPE'S PLEA TO WARRING NATIONS. The Pope, in an Easter broadcast to the world yesterday, described the war as atrocious and appealed to the belligerents to refrain from using ' ever more deadly instruments of war.' ' Every new weapon of war,' he said, ' inevitably results in a counter-weapon, on the part of the adversary, of even greater effectiveness. Already to-day one must lament the fact that repeatedly the limits have been exceeded of what might be permissible in a just war. Would not an increasing embitterment in the use of means of attack soon transform the war into an inconceivable horror? Let us pray for a peace for all—not a peace of oppression and destruction of nations, but for a peace which, guaranteeing the honour of all the nations, may satisfy their vital necessities and the legitimate rights of all. To the Powers occupying territories of others during the war we say with all due consideration: Let your conscience and your honour guide you in dealing justly, humanely, and providently with the people of the occupied territory."

MEXICO. As a sequel to the Papal Encyclical on Mexico, summarized earlier in this book, the following may be quoted from the London Catholic weekly the *Universe*, January 31, 1941: " *Freedom Returns to Mexico.*—President Camacho has aroused new hopes of religious freedom in Mexico, which may be directly concerned in the special session of Congress which he has summoned to consider a number of new Bills sponsored by his Government. A number of articles of the Constitution are to be amended, including article five, which among other matters decreed the prohibition of religious [monastic] vows and of monastic Orders. One of the principal subjects for discussion is the future of education, which at present must be ' socialist ' in the primary and other schools. The Minister of Education has announced already that the State cannot allow the teachers' organization to dictate their own ideas on political matters. The use of strikes as a political weapon is also to be forbidden, and the Government has already taken action against such strikes in the civil service and in the cinema industry."

THE POPE AND STATE TOTALITARIANISM. After the collapse of Germany and the end of the European part of " World War Two," the Pope uttered a vehement denunciation of State autocracy :—

PIUS XII, Allocution *Nell'Accogliere* (dealing with National Socialism; Address to the Sacred College of Cardinals; June 2, 1945): "After," said the Pontiff, " almost six years, the fratricidal strife has ended—at least, in one part. Peace (if one may so style it) is very frail, and calls for constant care if it is to last." " Christ, our Divine Lord, said that all who took up the sword unjustly would perish by the sword (Matt., xxvi, 52). And do we not see, this day, the consequences of a political theory and action which took no account of the holiest feelings of mankind, and which trampled down the principles of Christianity? The world sees with horror the resultant ruin." " For over twelve years," he continued, " We lived in Germany, and, so far as we had freedom in the existing

conditions, We strove to establish the rights of German
Catholicism. Thus We were able to assess the great
qualities of the nation, and We met its best personalities.
We felt sure that the diabolical phantom of National Socialism eventually would be cast off, the guilty punished, and
Germany rise again in glorious new vitality. For a time
We hoped that the [Nazi] movement might take a more
moderate and less calamitous direction; and in 1933 the
German Government offered to conclude a Concordat, the
suggestion being supported by the German bishops, and a
majority of German Catholics. . . . The Church was not
misled by excessive hope; neither, in agreeing to a Concordat, did she at all give her approval to the teachings and
tendencies of National Socialism. This was definitely made
clear." " The Concordat secured for a time some advantages, or delayed some evils; [but] . . . the attacks on the
Church grew more violent. Catholic organizations were
dissolved; Catholic schools suppressed; young people
forced from home and Church; . . . the Catholic Press was
prohibited. To meet these assaults brave Catholics rallied
round their bishops. . . . The Holy See repeatedly pro-
tested to the German Government." " When, however,
all other means had failed, . . . he [Pius XI] issued the
Encyclical *Mit Brennender Sorge*, unmasking the real nature
of National Socialism. . . . Many people, hitherto—even
beyond Germany—blind to the contradiction between
National Socialist ideals and Christian teaching, now saw
and admitted their error." " The Church at least cannot be
reproached for not having warned against the real character
of the National Socialist movement, and the danger of it to
Christian culture." " On the side of those whom the
Encyclical assailed, there was an inevitable reaction, and
1937 was for German Catholicity a period of suffering and
terrible persecution. . . . [The Nazis] flattered themselves

that—when they had been victors in the war—they would be able to finish off the Church." " Providence, however, had disposed otherwise. The woes of the Church at the hands of National Socialism have ended in the sudden and dramatic end of the persecutor." At the conclusion of his Address the Pope said: " The way to a real, genuine pacification will be—We gave this warning a little time since—long and hard: too hard and long for the patience of mankind, which thirsts for order and peace. But perhaps this inevitable tardiness may be the better way. The storm of passions must be given time to die down: *Motus praestat componere fluctus* (Vergil, *Aeneid*, i, 135). Hate, lack of mutual confidence, feelings of excessive nationalism, must be replaced by wise counsels, by peaceful plans, by a quiet exchange of views, and by fraternal understandings."

WOMEN IN PUBLIC LIFE. On October 21, 1945, Pope Pius XII gave an address to the Catholic Women's Associations:—

PIUS XII, Allocution (*Questa grande vostra Adunta*, " On Women's Duties in Social and Political Life "). " In our opinion," he said, " the problem of woman comes to that of safeguarding and heightening her God-given dignity. Therefore it is not merely juridical, economic, educational, biological, or demographic. It amounts to asking: How is her God-given dignity to be kept and increased?" " A woman's natural function is to be a mother." Some, however (either voluntarily or by force of circumstances), do not have that vocation: Yet they may have a true form of motherhood " in a spiritual and more exalted sense." Women, however, must beware of false advisers: " A certain totalitarian regime offers her ' equal rights ' with men. . . . We Ourselves have insisted that women's wages, when they do the same tasks as men, should be the same as men's. . . . Yet the query still emerges:

Are woman's conditions improved? 'Equal rights with men' has led to desertion of homelife." "Restore woman to her honoured place as housewife and mother." "Some wives, to increase the domestic income, work in factories and neglect the home." This leads to grave evils: on which the Pope dwelt in some detail; then he said: "Do We therefore find it needful that Catholic women and girls should refuse the trend to social and political life? No!—for a surety, no! . . . Often the absence from home is due not to 'emancipation' theories, but to necessity—the need for daily bread." This is a product of bad social conditions; therefore: "Would you Catholics leave to other women—to those, even, who are conniving at the ruin of the home—the monopoly of organizing social affairs?" The task of entering public life is especially laid on Catholic unmarried women: "those on whom circumstances have imposed a mysterious vocation, destining them to a life of solitude which they did not desire, and which might lead to a useless, motiveless existence." To them "is opened a spacious field of work. . . . To study and expound woman's place and function in the community; her obligations and claims; to be guide to other women; to correct wrong theories, dissipate prejudices, clear up confusions; to explain and spread Catholic doctrine, as the best way to defeat error, illusions, and falsehood." "No wise woman is in favour of class-war or belligerency. When she votes, she should support peace, and oppose any tendency—from whencesoever—that subordinates the internal or external peace of the nation to any egoistically ambitious seekers of domination. Bravely, then, Catholic women and girls, labour without ceasing, heedless of difficulties and obstacles. Under the ensign of Christ the King, and with the patronage of the Mother Most Admirable, Queen of Mothers, work to restore the home, family, and society!"

A Maltese Prosecution

The following legal report is taken from the *Times of Malta*, November 13, 1946, page 8. It is given without comment except that (1) Malta, of course, is a part of the British Empire, and also is an intensely Catholic island; and (2) The intensity of its Catholicity is shown in this very issue of the *Times of Malta*, which carries an ecclesiological-historical article, "The Islet of Filfla," by the Rev. Loreto Zammit; a "St. Anthony of Padua Contribution List"; a report of the bringing of the Relics of St. Anthony to Gozo; and a notice of a prospective Augustinian pilgrimage. The legal report is as follows:—

"Law Report.—H.M.'s Criminal Court of Appeal. Profanity and Scurrility. *Police v. Joseph Farrugia. Before Mr. Justice W. Harding. Sitting on October* 29, 1946. Farrugia, on August 20, 1946, was found guilty by the Judicial Police Court, of having repeatedly contravened Section 28 of the Post Office Act by sending impious articles through the post, and was sentenced to 15 days' imprisonment, the Court ordering the confiscation of the incriminating articles, which consisted of a number of books. He entered an appeal on various technical grounds, having admitted through his Defence Counsel that he had sent some of the books, exhibited in Court, by post and he had kept the rest in his possession.

"The Defence Counsel raised an initial point as to whether the offence should be considered a contravention barred by prescription, as it had been committed more than three months before the commencement of proceedings.

The plea was, however, rejected, the Appeal Court holding that since the punishment of imprisonment with the alternative of the imposition of a fine (multa) was awarded for the offence, this could not be considered a contravention (F. Azzopardi vs. Dr. Mizzi—Civ. App. 9/11/1917; Pol. vs. Gatt; Pol. vs. Vella; Pol. vs. Mifsud—Crim. App. 27/3/42, 26/11/43, and 9/2/44).

"Another Defence plea, questioning the applicability of the Revised Edition of the Laws of Malta on the ground that these had not been published at the time the offence was committed, was also rejected by the Appeal Court, which quoted from Sir Allison Russell's ' Legislative Drafting and Forms ' to show ' that the publication of a Revised Edition is only intended to make available in convenient form all the statute law that is really living, and no more, and to clear up difficulties in what James I called " divers cross and cuffing statutes, and some so penned that they may be taken in divers, yea contrary senses." ' The Governor's Proclamation dated January 17, 1946, merely asserted that the authentic text of the law was that of the Revised Edition.

" The Appeal Court, considering what constituted ' impious articles,' observed that, for the purposes of the section of the law dealing with the offence, *impious* was a synonym of *blasphemous*. To show the correctness of this interpretation a quotation was made from Starkie to the effect that:—' The first grand offence of speech and writing in speaking blasphemously against God, or reproachfully concerning religion, with an intent to subvert man's faith in God or to impair his reverence of Him. Blasphemies against God and Religion may be regarded, spiritually, as acts of impious and imbecile hostility against the Almighty, or, temporally, as they affect the peace and good order of civil society. It is in the latter relation only that such offences are properly cognizable by municipal laws.

" ' To attempt to redress or avenge insults to a supreme and Omnipotent Creator would be absurd; but when it is considered that such impieties not only tend to weaken and undermine the very foundation on which all human laws must rest, and to dissolve those moral and religious obligations without the aid of which mere positive laws and penal restraints would be inefficacious, but also immediately tend to acts of outrage and violence—being, for the most part, gross insults to those who believe in the doctrines which are held up to scorn and contempt—they necessarily become an important subject of municipal coercion and restraint. Offences of this nature are punishable in the temporal courts with fine and imprisonment because they tend to subvert all religion and morality, which are the foundation of Government.'

" Having established that ' impiety ' and ' blasphemy ' carried the same significance in law, the Appeal Court examined the full meaning of blasphemy. The case of Rex vs. Taylor was quoted, a case in which the incriminating phrase had been ' Religion is a cheat.' Sir Matthew Hale had commented on this phrase, saying that ' Such kind of wicked, blasphemous words were not only an offence to God and Religion, but a crime against the laws, State, and Government, and therefore punishable in this Court, for to say " Religion is a cheat " is to dissolve all those obligations whereby civil society is preserved, and Christianity is parcel of the laws of England, and therefore to reproach the Christian Religion is to speak in subversion of the Law.'

" In Rex vs. Woolston, Chief Justice Raymond had said : ' Christianity in general is parcel of the Common Law of England, and therefore to be protected by it. Now, whatever strikes at the very root of Christianity, tends manifestly to a dissolution of the civil government. I would have it taken notice of that we do not meddle with any differences of

opinion and that we interfere only when the very root of
Christianity is struck at . . .'

" In Bowman vs. Secular Society Ltd., decided by the
House of Lords, Lord Buckmaster had stated: ' Assuming
that the object of the Society involved is a denial of Christianity, it was not criminal, inasmuch as the propagation of
anti-Christian doctrines, apart from scurrility and profanity,
did not constitute the offence of blasphemy. . . . Blasphemy is constituted by violent and gross language, and
the phrase, " reviling the Christian Religion," shows that
without vilification there is no offence.'

" Thus, the Appeal Court held, two ingredients are
necessary for the commission of the offence, viz.:

" 1. The impious language must be directed against God,
the Holy Trinity, the Sacred Christianity in general or
Religion in general;

" 2. The language used must be profane or scurrilous,
abusive or intemperate, showing the intent of the offender
to hurt the religious feelings of others.

" Then the Court examined the incriminated books,
quoting various excerpts to show that the required ingredients of ' blasphemy and impiety ' existed therein.

" After registering certain extenuating circumstances,
the Court commuted the term of imprisonment into a fine
of £25, ordering that the books be confiscated and kept by
the Registrar in such a way that they could not reach any
third person."

Since this case, a Labour Government has come into
power in Malta; but all its members are Catholics. Malta
definitely upholds Catholicism by law.

A Few Papal Pronouncements on General Theological Subjects

The subject of this book is that of Papal teaching as to politics and sociology. It is therefore really outside our present object to examine such teaching on the more general problems of theology in its widest aspects. Such examination would be full of interest, for it would bring up a multitude of matters of deepest philosophic and religious importance, many of them fascinating to a degree: Scholastic philosophy; Church history; canon law; Biblical criticism and exegesis; the monastic Orders; the Papal attitude to schismatic Christian bodies; the history of Catholic " missions to the heathen "; the lives of martyrs and other devotees; the doctrine and practice of the Sacraments; liturgy; the controversies with Protestants and with modern scepticism; devotional and moral theology—the very number of the subjects makes it impossible to deal with them all in this book. There are a few, however, which must be considered, since they indicate the fundamental philosophical outlook of the Popes and therefore have an important bearing on their attitude to social and political matters.

The Bible. At the time of the Reformation, in the sixteenth century, it was taken for granted—at least, as a rule—that the Bible was divinely inspired in its entirety, infallibly true, and that it could be quoted to prove what are the correct Christian teachings. The only real Biblical matters in dispute were as to (1) What books made up the real Bible; (2) What was the true meaning of Biblical statements; and (3) Whether the historic Catholic Church should have the controlling voice in deciding what doctrines were true. Catholics held that the "Deuterocanon" (called by Protestants the "Apocrypha") is as much a part of Holy Writ as were the other books; and they asserted that the correct meaning of the Bible was to be decided by the traditional voice of the Church. Protestants differed from them as to these issues, but both sides accepted the belief that the Bible was inspired and devoid of error. This state of affairs, however, could not be permanent. Protestantism, by claiming the right of private judgment in opposition to the theory and doctrine of a dogmatically infallible Church, could not for ever refrain from challenging the authority of an assertedly infallible Bible. By the middle of the eighteenth century the criticism of the Bible had become insistent. By the middle of the nineteenth it had invaded the very citadels of the Protestants.

The Council of the Vatican in 1870—confirming the Council of Trent which in the sixteenth century had settled for Catholics the main questions in debate between them and Protestants—had decreed (Session 3, canon 2 *de Revelatione*): "The books of the Old and New Testament, whole and entire with all their parts, as enumerated in the decree of this same Council, and as they exist in the ancient Latin Vulgate, are to be received as sacred and canonical, not because, having been composed by human industry, they were afterwards approved by her authority; nor only because they contain Revelation without error; but because, having been written under the inspiration of the Holy Spirit, they have God for their author." The flood of Higher Criticism, however, could not fail, to an extent, to affect even some Catholic scholars, who tried to lessen the force of this belief. On November 18, 1893, therefore, POPE LEO XIII issued a memorable Encyclical (*Provi-*

dentissimus Deus: " On the Study of Holy Scripture "). He dwelt on the nature of Divine Revelation; the value of the Bible; and the fidelity with which the Church had kept and expounded the Bible. He described what he considered proper methods of interpreting Scripture and then came to the question of its inspiration and of the modern critical assaults on it. His decision was uncompromising. " We have to contend," he said, " against those who, making an evil use of physical science, minutely scrutinize the Sacred Book in order to detect the writers in a mistake." After having quoted the statements of Fathers of the Church, and the decrees of the Councils of Trent and the Vatican, he said: " It follows that those who maintain that an error is possible in any genuine passage of the sacred writings, either pervert the Catholic notion of inspiration, or make God the author of such error." This position of Leo XIII was maintained by Pius X in 1907 in his Encyclical *Pascendi*, " On Modernism " *; by Benedict XV in 1920 in *Spiritus Paraclitus*; and by Pius XII in 1943 (*Divino Afflante*). All Catholics, therefore, must believe that in *the genuine text* of the Bible there are no *formal* errors of any kind. Catholic scholars may inquire whether any passage which presents an apparent difficulty is a real part of the original text, or, if so, whether it is a formal statement as to fact or only a report of what someone said. Also, allowances may be made for " popular modes of expression," for figurative language; and so on. On these subjects the Catholic view may be seen well expressed in three 3d. pamphlets of the Catholic Truth Society, London, by the Rev. C. L. Lattey, S.J.: *The Truth of Scripture, Prophecy*, and *Revelation*. The basic fact remains, however, that Catholics

* The word " Modernism " has obtained since then a wider meaning, but as used by the Pope it referred to a special movement amongst Catholics.

must hold the Bible's direct statements to be all true. The 1907 Decree *Lamentabili* (see later in this book) also seems to bar Catholics from most theories of the Higher Criticism.

Modernism. At the end of the nineteenth and the beginning of the twentieth century, in especially Germany, Italy, and England, a spirit had arisen amongst Catholics which sought to adapt the faith and practice of the Church to modern thought by explaining it in mystical senses.* This movement was silenced by the famous Encyclical of Pius X, *Pascendi Dominici Gregis* (" On the Doctrines of the Modernists "; September 8, 1907). It had been preceded by a declaration of the Holy Office, *Lamentabili Sane* (" Decree of the Holy Roman and Universal Inquisition, ' On Modernist Errors ' "; July 3, 1907). The decree said: " With truly lamentable results our age, intolerant of all control in its investigations of the ultimate causes of things, not infrequently follows what is new in such a way as to reject the heritage, so to say, of the human race, and thus to fall into most grievous errors. . . . Lest errors of this kind, which are being daily spread amongst the faithful, should strike root in their minds and corrupt the purity of the faith, it has pleased His Holiness Pius X, by Divine Providence Pope, that the chief amongst them should be noted and condemned through the office of this Holy Roman and Universal Inquisition. Wherefore, after a most diligent investigation, and after having taken the opinion of the Reverend Consultors, the Most Eminent and Reverend Lords Cardinals, the General Inquisitors in matters of faith and morals, decided that the following propositions are to be condemned and proscribed—as they are, by this General Decree, condemned and proscribed."

* The most notable English Catholic Modernist was Father Tyrrell, a Jesuit. He died excommunicated.

A list was then given of sixty-five propositions. Amongst them were: (1) The ecclesiastical law, which prescribes that books regarding the Divine Scriptures are subject to previous censorship, does not extend to critical scholars or students of the scientific exegesis of the Old and New Testaments. (2) The Church's interpretation of the Sacred Books is not indeed to be despised, but it is subject to the more accurate judgment and correction of the exegetes [scientific critics]. (3) From the ecclesiastical judgments and censures passed against free and learned exegesis [interpretation] it may be gathered that the faith proposed by the Church contradicts history, and that Catholic dogmas cannot really be reconciled with the true origins of the Christian religion. (4) The magisterium of the Church cannot, even through dogmatic definitions, determine the genuine sense of the Sacred Scriptures. (5) Since, in the deposit of the faith, only revealed truths are contained, in no way does it appertain to the Church to pass judgment concerning the assertions of human sciences. (6) In defining truths the ' teaching Church ' and the ' Church taught ' collaborate in such a way that the only function of the former is to sanction the common opinions of the latter. (7) The Church, when she proscribes errors, cannot exact from the faithful any internal assent to the judgments issued by her. (8) Those who treat as of no weight the condemnations passed by the Sacred Congregation of the Index, or by other Roman Congregations, are free from all blame. (9) Those who believe that God is really the author of the Sacred Scriptures display excessive simplicity or ignorance. (10) The inspiration of the books of the Old Testament consists in the fact that the Israelite writers have handed down religious doctrines under a peculiar aspect, either little or not at all known to the Gentiles. (11) Divine inspiration does not so extend to the whole of the Sacred Scripture as to render each and all of its parts immune from all error. (12) The exegete, if he wishes to apply himself usefully to Biblical studies, must first of all put aside all preconceived opinions concerning the supernatural origin of Sacred Scripture, and interpret it not otherwise than other merely human documents." Propositions 13 to 19 were theories put forward by Higher Critics about the New Testament. The rest of the propositions explained away dogmas as not literally binding; and Propositions 64 and 65 were: " (64) The progress of science demands that the concepts of Christian doctrine concerning God, Creation, Revelation, the Person of the Incarnate Word, Redemption, be recast; (65) Modern Catholicism cannot be reconciled with true science unless it be transformed into a non-dogmatic Christianity, that is into a broad and liberal Protestantism." The decree then brusquely ended: " And on the following Thursday, the fourth day of the same month and year, an accurate report of all this having been made to our Most Holy Lord Pius X, His Holiness approved and confirmed the Decree of the Most Eminent Fathers, and ordered that the propositions above enumerated, all and several, be held by all as condemned and proscribed.—PIETRO PALOMBELLI, Notary of the Holy Roman and Universal Inquisition."

The Encyclical *Pascendi* followed in two months, and a drastic document it was, bringing dismay to the ranks of Modernist Catholics:—

PIUS X, Encyclical *Pascendi Dominici Gregis* (" On the Doctrines of the Modernists "; September 8, 1907): " One of the primary obligations assigned by Christ to the office divinely committed to Us of feeding the Lord's flock (*pascendi Dominici gregis*) is," began the Pontiff, " that of guarding with the greatest vigilance the deposit of the faith delivered to the saints, rejecting the profane novelties of words and the gainsaying of knowledge falsely so called. There has never been a time when this watchfulness of the supreme pastor was not necessary to the Catholic body; for, owing to the efforts of the enemy of the human race, there have never been lacking ' men speaking perverse things ' (Acts, xx, 30), ' vain talkers and seducers ' (Titus, i, 10), ' erring and driving into error ' (2 Tim., iii, 13). It must, however, be confessed that these latter days have witnessed a notable increase in the number of the enemies of the Cross of Christ, who, by arts entirely new and full of deceit, are striving to destroy the vital energy of the Church, and, as far as in them lies, utterly to subvert the very Kingdom of Christ. Wherefore We may no longer keep silence, lest We should seem to fail in Our most sacred duty, and lest the kindness that, in the hope of wiser counsels, We have hitherto shown them, should be set down to lack of diligence in the discharge of Our office." The Pope then declares that these " partisans of error " are found in the very bosom of the Church, " and, lost to all sense of modesty, put themselves forward as reformers of the Church." " They proceed to diffuse poison throughout the whole tree, so that there is no part of Catholic truth which they leave untouched, none that they do not strive to corrupt." The Encyclical proceeded to analyse the impugned teachings. Agnosticism is declared to be their foundation: " According to this teaching human reason is confined entirely within the field of *phenomena*, that is to say, to things that appear: it has neither the right nor the power to overstep these limits." Hence it cannot be possible to know by reason the existence of God, and genuine Revelation is excluded. Religion is, by Modernists (says the Encyclical), explained as a human development by " vital immanence." Church dogma has been formed by natural evolution, based on individual experience. Faith and science do not touch each other: but, nevertheless (illogically) faith is subject to science. The Encyclical described how the Modernists apply these principles to Church doctrine and the Sacraments: also to the Bible and the Church's constitution. It says they would separate Church and State. They would regard Church censorship of scholars as tyranny. Yet they put themselves forward *as apologists*—defenders of Catholicism!—also as reformers! The Encyclical then comes to a solemn declaration: " And now, with Our eyes fixed upon the whole system, no one will be surprised that We should define it to be the synthesis of all heresies." This (? *ex cathedra*) condemnation is followed by an analysis of the causes and propaganda methods, of Modernism. " Their whole system . . . has been born of the union between faith and false philosophy." What, then, is to be done? The Encyclical enjoins " remedial measures ":—Scholastic Philosophy must be the basis of the studies in colleges for aspirants to the priesthood: but there must be adequately a place for the natural sciences. " Anyone who is found to be in any way tainted with Modernism " " is to be excluded without compunction " from the work of teaching. Men seeking to be priests must be examined carefully to see that they are not affected by Modernism. Catholics must not go to " civil universities " if Catholic ones are available. To students, no publications " savouring of Modernism " may be allowed. Bishops must censor vigilantly the reading of Catholics: they must " exert themselves to proscribe and put out of the reach of the faithful injurious books or other writings printed or circulated in their dioceses." They should watch " Catholic booksellers " to see they do not sell such evil literature. Great care must be taken before a Bishop gives the censorial *nihil obstat* (" permission to print ") to any book. Priests must not be editors without permission of the bishop: which permission " shall be withdrawn from any priest who makes a wrong use of it after having received an admonition." " We have already," continued the Pope, " mentioned congresses and public gatherings as among the means used by Modernists to propagate and defend their opinions. In the future, Bishops shall not permit congresses of priests except on very rare occasions." " Diocesan Vigilance Committees " must be set up " to watch most carefully for every trace and sign of Modernism." Finally, Bishops must report every three years to the Pope on the subject of " the doctrines that find currency among the clergy." The Encyclical ended:—

" Meanwhile, Venerable Brethren, fully confident in your zeal and energy, We beseech for you with Our whole heart the abundance of heavenly light, so that in the midst of this great danger to souls from the insidious invasions of error upon every head, you may see clearly what ought to be done; and labour to do it with all your strength and courage. May Jesus Christ, the author and finisher of our faith, be with you in His power; and may the Immaculate Virgin, the destroyer of all heresies, be with you by her prayers and aid. And We, as a pledge of Our affection and of the Divine solace in adversity, most lovingly grant to you, your clergy and people, the Apostolic Benediction. *Given at St. Peter's, Rome, on the eighth day of September, one thousand nine hundred and seven*, the fifth year of Our Pontificate.—PIUS X, POPE."

Reunion of Christians. For many years past there has been an increasing tendency amongst Christians outside the Catholic fold to lessen their differences and try to unite. In the Anglican Church this even led to efforts to approach the Roman Church with proposals for reunion. This effort elicited in 1928, from the then reigning Pope, a short but very vigorous Encyclical:—

PIUS XI, Encyclical *Mortalium Animos Nunquam* (" On Fostering True Unity of Religion "—*De Vera Religionis Unitate Fovenda*; January 6, 1928). The Pope praised the desire for quelling disputes, but added: " Yet, when there is a question of fostering unity among Christians, it is easy for many to be misled by the apparent excellence of the object to be achieved." " Fair and alluring words cloak a most grave error, subversive of the foundations of the Catholic faith." " No religion can be true save that which rests upon the revelation of God." This revelation is taught by the Catholic Church, whose doctrines are to be accepted entire; for: " Has not God revealed them all (*Nonne Deus illas omnes revelavit*)? " " Let our separated children, then, draw nigh to the Apostolic See, set up in the city which Peter and Paul, Princes of the Apostles, consecrated by their blood; . . . and let them come, not with any intention or hope that ' the Church of the Living God, the pillar and ground of the truth ' (i Tim., iii, 15), will cast aside the integrity of the Faith and tolerate their errors, but to submit themselves to its teaching and government."

During the 1939–1945 war, however, in England there were certain approaches of Protestants and Catholics for common social activity against the moral evils of the age. For example, the London Catholic weekly, the *Universe* (June 6, 1941), had an article headed " Anglicans, Methodists, Catholics, Get Together Again." It described a Bognor Regis meeting, under the auspices of the " Sword of the Spirit " (a movement initiated by Cardinal Hinsley, the then Archbishop of Westminster), to discuss those evils. A Methodist leader, an Anglican bishop, and a Catholic monk, spoke. Other meetings followed: but their basis seems to have been radically insecure. A *Universe* article (March 15, 1946) was headed: " Anglican Bishop hears Monsignor Knox say ' No ' to Christian Front Idea."

It reported a meeting at Carlisle, at which " the Anglican Bishop of Carlisle, Dr. Williams, with members of his Cathedral Chapter and several other Anglican and Nonconformist clergy, heard Mgr. Ronald Knox deny the possibility of any common front in defence of Christian philosophy." " Our [Catholics'] whole approach to the business of theology is different from theirs [' other Christian bodies ']."

The truth is, of course, that Catholics can " co-operate " with " other Christians " only with the express implication that they do so as essentially different from them in religious status, and as really desiring those " other Christians " to accept full Roman authority. As illustration of this we have reserved for the end of this book the following summary of a remarkable Encyclical published by Pope Pius XI, and which in strict chronological order should have come after the Encyclical *Ubi Arcano* (1922):—

PIUS XI, Encyclical *Quas Primas* (" On the Kingship of Christ " ; December 11, 1925). " In the first Encyclical Letter which We addressed at the beginning of Our Pontificate to the Bishops of the Universal Church, We referred," said the Pope, " to the chief causes of the difficulties under which mankind is labouring. And We remember saying that these manifold evils in the world were due to the fact that the majority of men had thrust Jesus Christ and His holy law out of their lives." Therefore the Pope had determined " to insert into the Sacred Liturgy a special Feast of the Kingship of Our Lord Jesus Christ." " Therefore, by Our Apostolic Authority We institute the Feast of the Kingship of Our Lord Jesus Christ, to be observed yearly on the last Sunday of the month of October." The Encyclical dwells on the Catholic doctrine of the deity of Christ; but it is also remarkable and significant for the repetition and emphasis with which it declares that, for the right ordering of human affairs, the Church should be reinstated as supreme. "If We ordain that the whole Catholic world shall revere Christ as King, We shall minister to the need of the present day, and at the same time provide an excellent remedy for the plague that now infects society. We refer to the plague of secularism. . . . The Empire of Christ over all nations was rejected. The right which the Church has from Christ Himself, to teach mankind, to make laws, to govern peoples in all that pertains to their eternal salvation: that right was denied. . . . We firmly hope, however, that the Feast of the Kingship of Christ, which in future will be yearly observed, may hasten the return of society to our loving Saviour." The struggle, then, in the view of the Popes, is between secular liberalism, or secular sociological philosophy, and the ideal of the Church to be regarded by individuals and nations as supreme teacher of revealed truth. That is the issue.

N.B. Since the above was written the Holy Office at Rome has issued a decree sternly censuring meetings of Catholics and non-Catholics on a theological basis; but the London *Catholic Herald* (June 11, 1948) says there is still room for conferences on " social, political, and cultural matters."

APPENDIX

SINCE the foregoing was written, developments have occurred in the sphere of world politics which have a bearing on the subject of this book, and to which, therefore, it may be useful to refer.

In August, 1947, an important exchange of letters passed between Pope Pius XII and President Truman, of the United States of America. The following comment is from the *Boston Daily Globe*, Friday, August 29:—

" Rome, August 28.—Pope Pius XII and President Truman have pledged one another mutual support in their struggle for peace and against a common unnamed foe, which evidently is Communist Russia. Two notes, probably the most important which have passed between the two men, were exchanged Tuesday. They were held up until to-day for simultaneous release in Washington and Rome. Mr. Truman prompted the exchange with a 1,300-word letter to the Pontiff in which he laid heavy emphasis on the need for the unity of ' the moral forces of the world ' in seeking to preserve peace. Pope Pius hinted in reply that there are some flaws in the moral position of the United States. He indicated further, however, that the American position has so much to recommend it that Mr. Truman's peace efforts ' will find wholehearted co-operation from God's Church.' "

On Sunday, September 7, Pope Pius XII addressed a great assembly gathered in St. Peter's Square, Rome.

Dwelling on the evils of the present-day he said: "There is no time to be lost. The time for reflection and planning is past. Now is the time for action. Are you ready? The opposing fronts in the religious and moral fields are becoming ever more clearly defined. The time of the test is here" (London Catholic weekly, the *Universe*, September 12, 1947).

On Friday, September 5, the Pope had received in private audience four American Baptist ministers, "who told him they defended the policies of President Truman, a fellow-Baptist" (*Universe*, September 12). Referring to these events, a London "moderate Low Church" weekly, *The Record*, September 12, said: "The march of Russian influence . . . calls for a crusade of all the forces of righteousness in an attempt to overwhelm the evil, and the strongest centre of this crusade at present is probably the Vatican." On the other hand, a less "moderate" Low Church paper, *The English Churchman* (same date), commented: "The movement that desires to see the Pope acclaimed as moral leader of the world is dangerous in the extreme."

On October 6, 1947, the Press announced the formation in Belgrade, under Russian Communist guidance, of an organization of "nine nations," "to contain [resist] American expansionism." The London *Daily Telegraph*, October 7, in a note from its Vienna correspondent, had this comment: "Formation of the Communist Bureau of Information in Belgrade is regarded by experienced observers of Eastern European affairs here as a first step in an all-out Communist drive to secure domination of Europe." In the London *News Chronicle*, October 7, the noted "columnist," Vernon Bartlett, wrote: "It is a return to the acceptance of Lenin's thesis that ' it is impossible to finish off Capitalism until we have finished off Social Democracy in the Working Class Movement.' "   The London *Catholic Herald*, October 3, lamented the participation of some Catholics in quasi-Fascist activities : " There is a danger of the Church in this country being accused of sponsoring Fascism."   The London *News Chronicle* and other papers, October 9, announced an American Government statement denouncing the new Russian move as " trying to prevent the economic recovery of Europe."

It seems clear that an " ideological antagonism of two blocs," if not definitely forming, is in prospect of such formation.   The consequences are incalculable.

Some Books Recommended

The following list is simply that of a few works, by writers or compilers of various views, which may be useful for further study :—

The Popes and the People (a collection of Papal Encyclicals, published by the Catholic Truth Society, London).
The Catholic Dictionary, by Addis and Arnold.
Lord of the World (novel by Robert Hugh Benson).
The Dawn of All (another novel by Benson).
The Decay of the Church of Rome, by Joseph McCabe.
The Gospels—Fact or Fiction?, by J. P. Arendzen.
Supernatural Religion, by W. R. Cassels.
Inside the Roman Church, by J. W. Poynter.

> (This should be read in comparison with the same writer's youthful work, *Rome, Christendom, and a ' League of Churches,'* published in 1919. It is now out of print, but is in the British Museum Library.)

The Catholic Church Against the Twentieth Century, by Avro Manhattan.
Christianity at the Cross-roads, by Father Tyrrell, the English Modernist of the times of Pius X's Encyclical *Pascendi*.
The Pope, by G. K. Chesterton.
How the Reformation Happened, by Hilaire Belloc.
Roman Catholic Claims, by Bishop C. Gore.
Bishop Gore and the Catholic Claims, by Dom J. Chapman.
The Rise of Christianity, by Bishop Barnes.
The Third Day, by Arnold Lunn.
The Protestant Dictionary (published by the Protestant Reformation Society, London).
The Background of the Bible (two vols.), by Archibald Robertson.
Gods Divide (novel by A. D. Howell Smith).
The Rise of the Spanish Empire, by Señor Madariaga.
The Light that has not Failed, by G. S. Oddie.
The Testament of Christian Civilization, by Joseph McCabe.
Parish Life in Mediaeval England, by Cardinal Gasquet.
The works of G. G. Coulton on Mediaevalism—many volumes.

Codex Juris Canonici (the Code of Roman Canon Law, published in 1917 by the Vatican Press, and available from all Catholic publishers. It is, of course, in Latin).

Praelectiones Theologicae, by Perrone (in Latin).

Grammar of Assent, by Cardinal Newman.

The Key to the World's Progress, by Charles Stanton Devas.

The Riddle of the Universe, by Ernst Haeckel; trans. by Joseph McCabe.

Haeckel's Monism False, by Frank Ballard.

Haeckel's Critics Answered, by Joseph McCabe.

Whom say Ye . . .?, by J. P. Arendzen.

The True Story of the Vatican Council, by Cardinal Manning.

The Popes and the Council, by " Janus."

Papal Infallibility, by Archbishop MacIntyre (Catholic Truth Society).

The Infallibility of the Church, by George Salmon.

A City Set on a Hill, by Robert Hugh Benson.

The Seat of Authority in Religion, by Martineau.

Vaticanism, by W. E. Gladstone.

Letter to the Duke of Norfolk on the Pope and the Council, by Cardinal Newman.

The Martyrdom of Ferrer (Barcelona riots of 1909), by Joseph McCabe.

The Catholic Church and the Principle of Private Property, by Hilaire Belloc (Catholic Truth Society pamphlet).

Merrie England and *Britain for the British* (Robert Blatchford's classic exposition of idealistic Socialism in the 1890's). Also his (later) novel on similar lines : *The Sorcery Shop.*

Aristocracy and Evolution, by W. H. Mallock (Anti-Socialist, 1898. It " dates," but is very able).

[Many of the above are out of print, but are in the British Museum Library. All (or most) are very useful, and repay consultation by those who can get access to that Library for consulting the works that are not otherwise obtainable.]